ARNOLD L. HASKELL

What is a Ballet?

Macdonald : London

First published in 1965 by
Macdonald & Co. (Publishers) Ltd.
Gulf House, 2 Portman Street,
London, W.1.

Made and printed in Great Britain by Tonbridge Printers Limited, Peach
Hall Works, Tonbridge, Kent.

TRIDENT BOOKS

General Editor: Sir William Emrys Williams, C.B.E., D.Litt.

WHAT IS A BALLET?

Other available titles in this Series

What is a Play? by Ivor Brown
What is a Film? by Roger Manvell

Contents

Illustrations

A NOTE ON THE PHOTOGRAPHS

I have thought it better, rather than to give a vast number of postage stamp size illustrations of the main events and personalities mentioned in this book, which in any case are easily accessible, to select photographs that give something of the atmosphere of ballet. I have in fact chosen photographs that give me particular pleasure in evoking memories of familiar scenes on stage, backstage and in school. Even the close-up of a 'ballet face' is valuable in this respect. I have a small bronze by Rodin, entitled *tête de danseuse*, it brings me in contact with a whole period of ballet in a way that many a slick and mechanically perfect action photo fails to do.

I am greatly indebted to my friend Mike Davis for the large collection of his photographs that he set aside for my choice, and to my friend and colleague Vera Roslavleva who collected pictures in the Soviet Union. My only difficulty was in making a selection.

The author and publishers wish to thank the following for supplying photographs: APN for 17; the Bakrushin Museum for 3; V. Bliokh for 13, 16; Coleccion Luis Angel Torres for 1; Mike Davis for 4, 5, 7, 8, 11, 14, 18, 19, 20; L. Dubilt for 15; M. Murazov for 10; U.S.S.R. for 2, 9; L. Zhdanov for 6, 12.

Dedication

For Joy and for Jacqueline and her Three Graces,
Christine, Charlotte, Elizabeth.

With love.

A. L. H.

A DIVERTISSEMENT BY WAY OF PROLOGUE

'Alas, I am obliged to explain to you by means of the written word exquisite dramas where no one utters a syllable and which, indeed, demonstrate the uselessness of words.'

Jules Lemaître

'Ballet expresses movements that painting and sculpture cannot, and through these movements it reveals the true nature of mind and matter.'

Father Menestrier

'Où les beaux vers, la danse et la musique, de cent plaisirs font un plaisir unique.'

Voltaire on ballet

'As an actress I salute dancers with the reverence of a man for his ancestors. The dancer is certainly the parent of my own art, but he has other children. All arts of which the special attribute is movement, descend from the dancer . . . dancing movements formed the first metres of true poetry.'

Ellen Terry

'The King desires to learn the whole meaning of art, but is told that he must first know the theory of dancing.'

quoted by *Stella Kramrish*
The Art of India

'My dance is also life, stripped of its accidental and irrelevant coverings.'

Pavlova

'Work does not only mean the work of your arms, your legs, your body. Naturally, the work of the mind and heart, the work of the spirit, is not the least of factors in what the ballet dancer does.'

Ulanova

Ballet Words

ABSTRACT Term loosely used to describe a ballet without theme or story. True abstraction cannot exist in ballet.

ADAGIO The high spot in a classical ballet where the ballerina, supported by her partner, reveals her line, musicianship and artistry. A slow movement in contrast to *allegro*.

ARABESQUE Possibly a term borrowed from Moorish art. A pose in which one leg is extended straight to the back and, most usually, the opposite arm is extended forward. There are a number of different arabesques. Restful for the eye to caress the gentle sloping line, and never monotonous because of the contrast of the angle formed by the legs.

ART DIRECTOR (French, *collaborateur artistique*). The person, so often missing today, whose function it is to blend the elements that go to make up a ballet. Diaghilev was the supreme art director.

ATTACK   Impact made by the total performance, as distinct from the linking together of steps.

ATTITUDE   A pose said to have been developed by Carlo Blasis and inspired by Gian Bologna's winged Mercury, in which one leg is raised at the back, bent at the knee. Usually the corresponding arm is raised.

BALLET   Read the text.

BALLET BLANC   A term that covers the romantic ballet danced in white tarlatan, ushered in by *La Sylphide* in 1832.

BALLET D'ACTION   Old term to distinguish the dramatic ballet from a *divertissement* (q.v.) or a *suite de danses* (q.v.).

BALLETOMANE   A term first used to denote the regular patrons of the Maryinsky Theatre, those with reserved seats who were 'in the know'. Introduced into English by the present writer, 1934.

BARRE   A fixed horizontal bar running parallel with the walls of the studio at about the height of the hips. The dancer begins his class with barre work, using the bar for balance.

BOLSHOI THEATRE   Founded in 1776. The Moscow Opera House.

12

CARACTÈRE Folk or traditional dance, or dance based on folk dancing. Broad comedy or *bouffe*.

CHOREOGRAPHER The inventor of the steps and movements of the ballet.

CLASSICAL BALLET Ballet that derives from the basic technique laid down by Blasis and modified in Russia by visiting and native teachers. It can also mean ballet that has been a long time in the repertoire, but this is misleading especially when such a ballet as *Les Sylphides* is intended. Such nomenclature infuriated Fokine, who led the revolt from classicism.

CORPS DE BALLET Members of the chorus, as distinct from principals and soloists. It can also mean the company as a whole.

CORYPHÉE (from the Greek – Koruphaios, chorus leader). A leading member of a *corps de ballet*. Curiously, this noun is masculine.

CRITIC An angel when he praises an artist, a villain when he dislikes her, and the very devil when he praises her rival. Has an important function in ballet, holding a watching brief for the totality of the arts, at times even defending ballet against the increasing monopoly of the dancers.

DANSEUR NOBLE The classical male dancer who enhances the effect of his ballerina partner by his nobility of manner and his modesty.

13

DEMI-CARACTÈRE The dance is based on the classical steps, but the character is not heroic and tends to be a *soubrette*, e.g., Swanilda in *Coppelia*.

DIVERTISSEMENT An entertainment arbitrarily composed of different dances, to be distinguished from a *suite de danses* (q.v.).

ENCHAÎNEMENT A series of steps linked together, c.f. sentences as opposed to words.

ENTRECHAT etymology much debated. It consists of a jump with feet crossed in front. Described in a book in 1725 but perfected by Camargo a few years later. Nijinsky is credited with the formidable number of ten. The *entrechat deux* is known as a *royale,* after Louis XIV.

FORMALISM Pattern for its own sake, divorced from emotional content. The use of dancers as puppets.

FOUETTÉ A whipping movement in which the dancer on her points whips out the working leg to the side and in to the knee with a slight circular movement. This is spectacular when combined with turns on the point in a fixed position on the stage. Once a rarity only performed by the Italians until learnt, amid national rejoicings, by the Russian ballerina, Kchessinska. It is a commonplace today.

FOYER DE LA DANSE An extension of the stage at the Paris Opera where the dancers warm up before a performance. It was a meeting place for the privileged, for purposes outside the concern of this book.

IMPRESARIO Used today to describe the business man who engages a company and launches a tour, rather than someone in the creative role of a Diaghilev.

LANGUAGE OF BALLET Since ballet grew up in France the language of ballet is French. This is used with varying accents easily understood by all throughout the studios and rehearsal rooms of the world, though sometimes confusing to the French themselves (Kooroo for couru!). It is not a sop to sentiment that has prevented these words from being translated. The reason is strictly practical. The writer has seen a Russian teacher take a class consisting of seventeen different nationalities without the need of translation. I have not included a general technical glossary. It would be meaningless unless set out at great length and with diagrams. A certain amount of ballet jargon, a technical term dropped here and there into the conversation, is a splendid one-upmanship gambit that would delight my friend Stephen Potter.

MAÎTRE DE BALLET Today indistinguishable from *régisseur* (q.v.). He sometimes takes company classes.

MARYINSKY THEATRE Opened in 1860. The St Petersburg Opera House, now called the Kirov, cradle of the Russian classical school.

MIME The conventional gesture language used in classical ballet.

15

MODERN DANCE Dance in a wide variety of different styles, using dancers not trained in the classical technique. Developed in Germany by Von Laban and Mary Wigman, and in the U.S.A. by Isadora Duncan, Ruth St Denis and Martha Graham. Its finest choreographer has been Kurt Jooss, creator of *The Green Table*.

NEO-CLASSIC BALLET The use of the classical technique divorced from the romantic story, greatly developed in the U.S.A. by Balanchine.

NEO-ROMANTIC BALLET the essence of romanticism without the romantic period accessories of mime, etc., the accent on expression rather than virtuosity, ushered in by Fokine, whose *Dying Swan* and *Les Sylphides* were manifestoes of the genre.

NOTATION the scoring of ballets through the use of symbols. Such systems include the Stepanov method, formerly used in Russia, the Laban method, and the Benesh method common in England today.

OPERA BALLET This must be distinguished from the opera ballet a stage in the development of the ballet and associated with Rameau in which the two arts were blended. It is Gluck who was responsible for creating opera in which ballet was an integral part of the action; e.g., the dances in Hades in *Orpheus and Eurydice*. Many operas have had ballets inserted as a condition of their performance as Grand Opera in Paris; they then become a break for the mythical 'tired business

16

1. Anna Pavlova in *The Dying Swan*
2. Galina Ulanova as Juliet (U.S.S.R.)

3. George Balanchine in his early days in Russia, from the portrait by Serebriakova (*courtesy Bakrushin Museum*)

man'. The Walpurgis Night in Faust, for instance, has even less connection with *Faust* than the rest of the opera. Ballet in opera is difficult to produce since the physical contrast between dancers and singers always produces something of a shock. It requires the most tactful handling so as to become a part of the action, and the dancers are more a scenic background and not the personalities of ballet proper; a fact that they sometimes resent.

The perfect opera ballet is the Polovtsian dances from *Prince Igor* where singers and audience are watching a spectacle that belongs to the narrative.

PERSONALITY A rare attribute, recognised when seen, though mannerisms can sometimes deceive the few.

PIROUETTE a turning of the body on point or half point of one foot while the other remains in the air. There are a number of different pirouettes.

PRIMA BALLERINA (or BALLERINA alone). The leading woman dancer who acts the heroines of the classical-romantic ballet. When she completely dominates the company she is called *prima ballerina assoluta*. Her male opposite number is known as a *premier danseur; ballerino* is no longer in use.

PROPAGANDA The subject of propaganda in ballet is often raised nowadays when dealing with such Soviet works as *The Red Poppy* or *The Path of Thunder*.

Propaganda in ballet is nothing new. There is an outstanding example from 1641, when *Le Grand Ballet de la Prosperité des Armes de la France* was shown as a warning to some Dutch envoys who were also issued with some descriptive written material. Miracle plays and the lavish ballets mounted by the Jesuits were also propaganda. It is not always easy to see where propaganda begins. It is natural for ballet to reflect the climate of opinion of the place in which it originates. The French Revolution (*The Flames of Paris*) and the Slaves Revolt (*Spartacus*) are obvious subjects for Soviet Ballet. In Russia deliberately aimed propaganda ballet would soon bore the public, as in a recent example, attacked and ridiculed by *Pravda,* which wrote, 'There is great need for music and choreography built around present day themes but a ballet featuring a *Superphosphate dance* is going a little too far.'

In one respect propaganda in the sense of a struggle between good and evil is the basic material of the theatre; when other people's good triumphs we call it propaganda.

RAT   (Les Petits Rats). Nickname for the junior members of the corps de ballet in Paris, immortalised in paintings and drawings and sculpture by Degas. Origin; from the deep cellars of the Opera? Because they are always nibbling sweets?

REALISM   The truth or plausibility of the action on the stage after it has been translated into choreographic terms. Not to be confused with *naturalism*, the raw material.

REGISSEUR   The stage manager who rehearses works already in the repertoire.

REVIVAL   This does not always imply what it would seem. It can mean a reproduction, a complete restaging, or a new ballet on an old story with possibly new music, e.g. Ashton's *Ondine*.

ROMANTIC BALLET   This refers to subject matter rather than technique, though it had many technical repercussions.

RUSSIAN BALLET   an often misused term, describing at times a company whose closest link with Russia was a dancer from St Petersburg, Florida. It is a trade mark for the school of ballet, developed in Russia. Today it can only be applied to companies in the Soviet Union. In England from 1910 until Hitler's war it meant the émigré Russian Ballets of Serge Diaghilev and Colonel de Basil.

SCHOOL   This means what it says, but *school,* in italics, denotes a particular use of the classical technique, either national or referring to some special teacher, e.g., Cecchetti. The differences are small, the nomenclature tends to vary but much heat is engendered by heresy hunting.

'SECOND'   There are no second Nijinskys, Pavlovas or Karsavinas. Their successors must be originals.

SUITE DE DANSES A series of dances by one composer in contrast to a *divertissement* (q.v.). e.g., *Les Sylphides*.

TEMPERAMENT Sometimes misused to describe such bad manners as slapping the stage manager, or in praise of a non-Spanish dancer stamping and sweating her way through a flamenco dance. On the stage it means giving the impression that the ballet is actually happening for the first time and is not a carefully rehearsed event. The dancer of temperament has true attack.

TERPSICHORE Greek muse of the dance, definitely a more picturesque figure than our patron saint, Vitus.

TERRE À TERRE literally 'earth to earth' as opposed to the virtuosity of elevation, this may be compared to the dramatic as opposed to the coloratura soprano.

TRAVESTI The *danseuse en travesti* wears allegedly male clothes and partners the female. Extinct today.

TUTU The short tarlatan ballet skirt used in classical ballet. Originally a slang term, but now a dictionary word. The correct name, largely obsolete, is *juponage*.

VARIATION A solo dance. The classical pas de deux has a variation for both dancers.

1 : *Prehistory*

Shiva, the dancing God

The dance is the original art form, man's first means of self-expression. It is of considerable importance to examine this bold claim before giving any outline of the history of ballet as we know it today, or attempting a study of its aesthetics.

It is significant that the Hindus represented Shiva, under one of his greatest names *Nataraja,* as a dancer whose rhythmic motions created and could destroy the universe. 'Our Lord,' says an ancient text, 'is the Dancer, who like the heat latent in firewood, diffuses His power in mind and matter and makes them dance in their turn.' This myth represents a profound truth. Dancing and movement are not synonyms. *Dancing is movement governed by rhythm.* The motions of the planets and the tides, the pulse beat in man, all bear witness to the truth of this conception of the dancing god, Shiva.

Western thought moves in a similar direction. 'It would seem that dancing came into being at the beginning of all things and was brought to light together with Eros, that ancient one . . .' wrote Lucian (A.D. 125).

Man's first means of expression is to dance in order to influence nature in his favour. It is a part of the instinct of self-preservation. This magic dance, therefore, being all important, must be governed by a definite set of rules. It is a ritual, that, when carefully observed, will bring good fortune in the hunt, death to tribal enemies and, later in the pattern of civilisation, good crops and fertility. It will accompany man in every phase of his existence; from birth and the difficult passage through adolescence to full membership of the tribe, and finally in his journey from this life to the next. It will protect the living from the lures of the dead. And, because man has faith in what he is doing, it is of immense practical value. It gives him power, courage and address in hunting and war. It frightens his enemies, as anyone who has seen a Maori or Zulu war dance can readily imagine; the very earth trembles under the plumed warrior's stamping feet. It dulls his pain. It gives him a good conceit of himself when it illustrates the history of his tribe and its descent from the elements, a snow capped mountain, or from some cunning and powerful jungle beast.

Such dance magic can take many forms, from the crude strength of the dancer in the rock cave or the jungle clearing, to the infinite subtleties of the Hindu sacred dances or our own high mass; the comparison was made by Monsignor Ronald Knox. The power of the dance comes down to us through time from the hysteria-induced dance epidemics of the Middle Ages or, for that matter, of our own days, even though these are fostered by the big business propaganda machine, to the moving performance of a great dancer at Covent Garden or the Bolshoi.

Ballet today is a highly stylised art whose history and aesthetics we shall examine in some detail, but if we forget this basic element of magic, we get an incomplete picture. We are not concerned with an entertainment but an art. The art, however, must entertain in order to survive; a magic that bored its practitioners would soon fail in its object.

The magic dance survives today in the rapidly narrowing areas where Stone Age man still dwells, only to be wiped out overnight once the explorer, the missionary, and the trader have passed. Sometimes its temporary survival takes on new forms, as when some aborigines near Darwin were seen to mime and dance a dog fight between Japanese Zeros and Spitfires, tacked on to one of their own tribal ceremonies. They had annihilated time. Indeed, were our own civilisation to be wiped out the magic dance would be instantly reborn, so pressing is the psychological urge. The normal man in the street, if he exists, invents his own private and compulsive rituals; the tapping of every fifth railing, or hopping from one paving stone to another, avoiding the joins. Golding has shown this deep need for magic in his remarkable novel *Lord of the Flies*. The neo-paganism of Nazi Germany saw a revival of such mystic power ceremonies called 'party rallies'. They took the familiar form of rituals where the high priest-leader poured power into his followers and in his turn received power from them, while lust for killing was whipped up by the rhythmic chanting of *Sieg Heil*, the clapping of hands, the waving of banners, and the stamping of the jackbooted brown shirted hoodlums. This word *power* is important in any writing on the dance, even, as we shall see, in the gentle art of ballet. Dance rhythm is hypnotic and infectious. This whole subject deserves very careful study at a period when so much attention has been paid to 'brain washing'.

The folk dance that ushers in a higher stage of civilisation has a different motivation, that of pleasure for the performer himself through joining in a social act. There is not always a sharp dividing line between the motives. At times the old magic dance persists when belief in the magic has worn thin, or even though the origin of the dance is no longer known to its exponents. After a time man has ceased to dance to bring about a good harvest; he still dances but as a relaxation after the hard work in the fields, in order to use muscles in play instead of in strain. New motives are awakened; the dance is a sport, the dance accompanies and eases work, its form often suggested by the nature of the work. The dance is an opportunity for courtship and social intercourse, the very pattern of the dance is important for its own sake and not for what it can accomplish. Already we are coming closer to our art of ballet, until at a certain moment in history this social dance becomes ballet.

At the present moment we can watch much the same thing happening as it did in the past. If we look at our ballroom dance, so popular on television, we have in the formation-dance an admirable example of this changeover. Here the complexities of step and pattern and the need for considerable rehearsal, show that the intention has been to entertain an audience. The same is the case with the many dance companies promoted by the various Peoples' Republics, the most notable being the Moiseyev ensemble from the U.S.S.R. Here a very rich folk dance has been choreographed and performed for an audience by a group of superlatively skilled ballet-trained dancers. This is the pattern that we shall see throughout our story, from mysticism to recreation, from the recreation of the amateur to the performance of the professional in front of an audience. Economics are as greatly involved as psychology.

The difficulty is to know exactly where to begin. There have been professional dancers since recorded history. Egypt had its professional 'cabaret' dancers. Salome took the place of a professional entertainer in that most notorious dance in all history. Greek dancers saw the birth of theatrical art. Roman mimes were the popular stars of their day, oriental dancers from the Eastern Empire originated the 'strip tease'.

The advent of Christianity came near to abolishing the dance, which was only excused by the invocation of various biblical texts that assured the faithful that dancing round the heavenly throne was the normal pursuit of the angelic host. Throughout history there has existed a love hate relationship between church and dance. In 774 an interdict was placed on religious dancing, in 1562 the fathers of the Council of Trent offered a ball to the ladies of the city. The Jesuits welcomed and used ballet, other orders condemned it.

Ballet A Living Language

One of the important things about the complex technique of ballet is the fact that it was not suddenly invented for some particular purpose by a select committee of savants. It developed, like a language, gradually, and, indeed, it is a true language of movement with its vocabulary, its grammar and its syntax. Hence the importance of some notion of its pre-history. Also, like a true language, it continues to develop. Modern dancers who are fluent in speech and in writing are never tired of affirming that they have found it inadequate to express certain current ideas and emotions, and that in consequence they have devised systems of their own, a sort of Esperanto. It is to be noted that their many systems have in a remarkably short time developed more *clichés* than ballet at its worst. They seem to excel in morbid subjects, lacking lightness and gaiety. They are basically untheatrical. Fokine attacked them for their lack of versatility. Ulanova says that 'without perfect mastery of the classics one cannot master new methods and expressive means of the dance.'

A pioneer in this new language was Isadora Duncan. She was an individualist and a rebel touched with genius. She invoked the spirit of Greek vase paintings and bas reliefs but, in fact, her dancing was probably further from Greece than the ballet technique from which she rebelled. In spite of her genius, the same thing applies to her as to the many others in Germany and the U.S.A., such as Mary Wigman and Ruth St Denis, who followed her lead. It is true that she came at a period, the beginning of the twentieth century, when

26

the balletic language was being used inadequately, and her revolt drew attention to this. The lesson was learnt in St Petersburg by Benois, Diaghilev, Fokine and their entourage, though they were already working on parallel lines. To serve this warning was not the least of her triumphs. Her failure and the failure of all the so called 'modern' dancers is that their language is too personal and restricted, that they attempt to express many things that cannot be expressed in movement, and that they have no consistency, so that they can on occasions move one to tears, but unfortunately also to laughter for the wrong reason. They lack a sense of proportion as do so many 'modern' artists in other media, through having no accepted discipline against which to measure themselves. The ageing Duncan was a battered ruin, the ageing Pavlova, diminished in the quantity of her technique was still superb in quality. Most important of all, they cannot transmit a living language to their pupils. In fact, Esperanto and other *ad hoc* languages are not capable of producing a literature. Their mission, and it is a valuable one, is to shame ballet into using its own language to the full, and also to enrich the ballet vocabulary in the way that the slang of yesterday is the highly respectable dictionary word of today. No, the word *slang* in this connection does not provide an exact parallel; the Charleston and the Twist provide our slang. It would be more accurate, in fact an exact parallel, to compare the modern dance movement to such linguistic experiments as James Joyce's *Anna Livia Plurabelle* or to the works of Gertrude Stein. The mention of modern dance at this stage is no digression. The conception of ballet technique as an organic language

27

is essential to any understanding of all that follows.

We start our story of ballet, therefore, with a rich and largely hidden pre-history, the main lines of which I have tried to suggest.

I am not going to do more in the chapters that follow than give a rough sketch of ballet history. Not only is there insufficient space, but many admirable and easily available histories exist. All that I intend to do is to deal with those features in the past that explain and illustrate the title of this book, 'What is a Ballet?'

2 : *The Birth of Ballet (Historical)*

The Journey from Italy to France

BALLET in the form that we recognise it today is essentially a product of the Italian Renaissance. When we compare a Byzantine Madonna and Child with one by Raphael, we have an immediate and a vivid visual impression of the change in atmosphere, and we are dealing with a visual art. After the Middle Ages the human body was no longer suspect; fragments of Greek and Roman sculpture were studied and collected, and the artist was allowed to depict pagan subjects.

Not only was the spiritual climate ready to nurture the new art, but the social, political and economic conditions were just right. Princes of highly cultivated tastes with money in their treasure chests gathered round them the greatest artists of a golden age, artists excited by the new spirit of humanism and the countless discoveries and opportunities that awaited them. And these Princes vied with one another in the quality and quantity of their pageantry. 'Keeping up with the Medicis' was the forcing house of ballet as it was of all the arts.

These gala performances were lavish pageants, at times equestrian, at times part banquet part entertainment, consisting of dancing and mime, singing and declamation loosely connected by some mythological theme. They contained the embryo of ballet, opera and the poetic drama. The words *entrée* and *entremets* in a menu originate from the various entrances of the performers and the danced intervals between the banquet courses. The costumes and the three dimensional décors, ingeniously contrived by painters who were also master stage engineers, were on a lavish scale. Leonardo designed many such fêtes at the court of Milan.

One of the greatest of these galas was held in 1489 in Tortona. A man of wealth, Bergonzio di Botta, gave a feast in honour of Gian Galeazzo Sforza, Duke of Milan, and his bride Isabella of Aragon. The danced interludes between the courses told the story of Jason. The dancers were the court nobles, and the dancing an extension of the court dances of the day.

It was Catherine de Medici who, when she became Queen of France and the mother of three kings, transplanted these entertainments from her native Florence. Brantôme tells us that she herself was a choreographer. It is said that she cultivated the enthusiasm of her sons, so that she herself could rule more freely.

Some historians date the birth of ballet from October 15th, 1581, when Catherine sponsored a performance to celebrate the marriage of the Duc de Joyeuse to

Marguerite de Lorraine. This is the first such performance to have a printed record. It was called *Le Ballet Comique de la Reyne*, and had as its subject the freeing of Ulyssess from the wiles of Circe, possibly a thinly veiled allegory since the Duc de Joyeuse was one of Henri III's *mignons*.

The whole entertainment was devised by Catherine's court musician, an Italian, Baldassarino de Belgiojoso (known in France and to posterity as Balthazar de Beaujoyeulx). His definition of his work is of particular interest, 'A geometrical arrangement of many persons dancing together under a diverse harmony of instruments.' It would describe many ballets at the present day.

The ballet closely reflected not only the customs and love intrigues of the court but also the politics of the day. This is admirably illustrated by many anecdotes.

When a courtier who was rehearsing a ballet fell out of favour with the Queen Regent, a number of the dancers felt it prudent not to turn up to rehearsal. The Prince was furious and said to Sully, 'I see you wish to turn my ballet into an affair of state'.

'No sir,' replied Sully, 'the contrary is the case. I consider your affairs of state a ballet'. The great Marshal of France, Francis de Bassompierre (1579–1646) owed his first promotion at court to his proficiency as a dancer. So keen he was that at the siege of La Rochelle he sent a despatch to the King: 'The scenery and the dancers are ready, the ballet can now begin.'

These dancer-courtiers must have been difficult to handle at times. When Crillon was taking lessons his teacher said. *'Pliez, reculez'*. 'No,' he replied, 'a Crillon

31

does not bend or retreat'.

In England the court masque was introduced from Italy by Henry the Eighth; Ben Jonson and many other distinguished poets subsequently wrote the libretti.

The steps of these dances survive, and can be reproduced from a famous book *Ochésographie*, written in 1588 by a distinguished cleric Jehan Tabouret, Canon of Langres, under the name Thoinot Arbeau. Arbeau gave much valuable advice, such as, 'Don't spit too much, don't blow your nose, don't land after a leap like a sack of corn'.

The association of Church and ballet has always been a close one, in spite of occasional rifts. The Jesuits used ballet to a considerable extent in their education, just as the baroque was a Jesuit art.

Such spectacles persisted for another century, limited only by expense – Le Ballet Comique de la Reyne had cost 3,600,000 francs – and later degenerating through the bawdy taste of Louis XIII. His taste may be excused by his sense of humour. Having cut the salary of two of his dancer-musicians they appeared at a masquerade at his *petit coucher* in strange attire. When he questioned them they replied, 'Half a salary only rates half a costume'. They were promptly reinstated.

In 1632 an important development took place. The general public was allowed at times to watch what had been a private entertainment, and in 1636 a theatre, Le Palais Cardinal, was built, greatly modifying the pattern of the entertainments.

4. Margot Fonteyn and Rudolf Nureyev in Act I, *Romeo and Juliet* (*Mike Davis*)

5. Svetlana Beriosova in Nijinska's *Les Biches* (*Mike Davis*)

Ballet Becomes a Profession

Louis XIV is known as *Le Roi Soleil,* a name he was given after dancing the role of Apollo in *Le Ballet de la Nuit* in 1653 when he was fifteen years of age. His first role had been in *Cassandre,* two years previously. Louis was enamoured of ballet, had resisted Mazarin's influence towards the operatic side of the entertainment that bored both the King and his subjects, and had gathered round him a galaxy of artists. Among them Molière, Benserade, the poet Jean Baptiste Lully, and the dancing master Charles Louis Beauchamps. The latter was the King's constant companion and danced with him in many ballets.

A number of reasons were to turn what was a social occasion into a profession. The very popularity of the ballet, and Molière's inspired use of it, underlined the scarcity of skilled dancers. The King became more and more preoccupied with power politics and war. It has also been suggested that his growing corpulence made him sensitive to ridicule,* and that he took Racine's mockery of Nero in his *Britannicus* to refer to him. At any rate, in 1661 he established *L'Académie Royale de la Danse,* whose membership consisted of the dancing masters of the court and nobility under the chairmanship of Beauchamps. They were assigned a room at the Louvre, but they preferred the more homely atmosphere of a tavern, *l'Epée de bois.*

The preamble to the act, drawn up in the King's hand, reads as follows: 'Although the art of dancing has

---

* And well he might be when it is remembered that he uttered such lines as: 'Plus brilliant et mieux fait que tous les dieux ensemble La terre ni le ciel n'ont rien qui me ressemble.'

always been recognised as one of the most honourable and most necessary for the training of the body . . . many ignorant persons have tried to disfigure and to spoil it . . . so that we see few among those of our court and suite who would be able to take part in our ballets, whatever scheme we draw up to attract them thereto . . . Wishing to establish the said art in its perfection and to increase it as much as possible, we deemed it opportune to establish in our good town of Paris a Royal Academy of Dancing.'

Beauchamp and his colleagues being for the most part illiterate, left no written record, but they systematised technique and defined the five positions of the feet that are to this day the basis of ballet. I write *systematised* since a technique existed, one that was described in detail in fifty-four rules at the end of the sixteenth century by Fabritio Caroso of Sermoneta and Cesare Negri of Milan, and there had been others before them.

In 1669, eight years later, Louis established *L'Académie Royale de Musique*, and three years later attached to it a school for the teaching of ballet. The year 1672, therefore, seems to me the logical date for the birth of ballet. *L'Académie Royale de Musique et de Danse* in existence today as the Paris Opéra, is the original home of ballet throughout the world.

Further Development of Ballet

When ballet became a full-time profession instead of a leisure pastime for courtiers, two things happened; there was an enormous extension of technique and also much thought given as to the aims of that technique.

And always, as we shall see, there come periods when the two, the means and the end, are in conflict.

The first notable innovation brought about by Louis' school was the emergence of women dancers. Previously the court ladies had taken part in the ballets, but more as a decorative background. They appeared but they were not allowed to perform *le moindre flic-flac*. The female roles were taken by men just as in the Elizabethan theatre. The first ballet in which women performed was in 1681, Lulli's appropriately named *Le Triomphe de l'Amour*. Some of these ballets held at Versailles were given over a period of three days, their marvellous costumes designed by a great master, Jean Berain. The women were still greatly handicapped by their stately court costume. They showed grace rather than virtuosity. The original ballerina was Mlle. Lafontaine, the first of a long line to be named *la reine de la danse*.

During the same fruitful reign ballet greatly extended its scope. In 1708, at a memorable fête given at the *Nuits de Sceaux* by La Duchesse de Maine, la Prévost interpreted – without words – the last act of Corneille's *Les Horaces*. The audience is said to have been moved to tears, though at least one spectator left it on record that he found the poignant happenings of Greek tragedy ill suited to the dance.

In England, too, dramatic ballet was being developed by John Weaver, a much neglected figure in the history of the dance.

Costume has always played a major role in the development of dance technique, exercising a restricting influence, at any rate until the invention of theatrical tights by Monsieur Maillot in the nineteenth century. This innovation shocked the Church so greatly that for a long time flesh coloured tights were banned in Italy.

In the early years of the eighteenth century there appeared one of the major figures in our history. Marie Camargo made her Paris debut in 1726. She shortened the traditional skirt to ankle length and adopted a heelless slipper.* She was now able to perform steps of elevation hitherto only performed by men. The virtuoso ballerina was born. The fame of Camargo helped to resolve a bitter controversy between the partisans of Lulli and Rameau. The Lullistes supported the horizontal dance, largely dictated by the ballroom floor where the spectators viewed from above, the *ramistes* postulated a vertical dance of more brilliant execution. As a dancer Camargo carried ballet into the future.

Her great contemporary and rival, Marie Sallé, was also a pioneer. Her particular gifts illustrate another aspect of dancing, the *terre à terre,* in which mime and what the dance expressed were more important than virtuosity. She, too, attempted a major modification of costume, but it was nearly two centuries in advance of its time. In 1734, in London, she appeared in a ballet *Pygmalion* in flowing, Greek-inspired draperies, an attempt at the *realism* that is of the essence of ballet and which will be discussed at some length in a later chapter.

One whole aspect of ballet dancing could be said to be illustrated by the rivalry of Camargo 'the agile' and

---

* It became the fashion 'de se chausser à la Camargo,' and her bootmaker became a rich man.

Sallé 'the enchantress,' to be repeated later by Taglioni and Elssler. Very few have succeeded in combining both their qualities.

During this whole period dancers, male and female, continued to develop technique, which often, performed for its own sake, verged on the acrobatic, until some outstanding balletmaster called a halt and began to question the whole basis of the art.

This struggle between dance-drama and dancing for its own sake, what the Russian critics call *formalism,* continues to this day and generates considerable heat among the critics. Ballet can be confined to neither.

Ballet Dramatists

The most articulate of all writers on the dance and the greatest pioneer, although other contemporaries worked to the same end, was the ballet master Jean-Georges Noverre, born in Paris in 1727, died in 1810. He was an outstanding choreographer, the teacher of more than one generation of dancers, and a man of tremendous power who was convinced that he alone truly understood the aesthetics of ballet. This, together with his irascible nature, forced him to travel, much to the benefit of the art as a whole. While in London he had been greatly influenced by David Garrick, whom he could understand without knowing the language; a revelation in the possibility of expression: 'Garrick tore at the heart of the spectator and made him cry blood.'

The period of Noverre's greatest influence was in Stuttgart, in the service of the court of Württemberg, where in addition to his own company, dancers came from Paris and elsewhere to assimilate and spread his ideas. In 1760 Noverre published his *Lettres sur la danse et les ballets*. It is still, after two hundred years, the Bible of the choreographer and the critic, invoked more often in the U.S.S.R. today than any other work. And indeed Noverre was always held in such high esteem in Russia that the finest edition of the work was published in St Petersburg in 1803, in four quarto volumes at the express command of the Tsar, Alexander I.

Very briefly Noverre's thesis was as follows. Ballet had got out of hand. There was a complete reign of anarchy, the poet ignored the composer, the composer did not collaborate with the *maître de ballet,* who in his turn did not tell the painter of his intentions, while the machinist was only concerned with stage illusion. The dancers were only interested in virtuosity and the rapid execution of steps, which often the slow tempo of the music did not allow. All composition had been forgotten, and a number of less talented dancers clung to the scenery until they formed a part of it, they were known as '*les gardes côtes**'

Technique had advanced to such an extent that it had become mechanical and meaningless. Dancers turned, leapt and spun for the sake of turning, leaping and spinning until the mind reeled and one became dizzy. Technique is essential, Noverre insisted, but only when it is the servant and not the master. The dancer must use his skill to express the emotions and to illustrate some dramatic situation. Enough of steps and 'geometric patterns' for their own sake. The choreo-

* Compare with 'the dancers near the fountain' at a later date, see page 105.

grapher must observe nature and study man in all his moods. There must be consistency in the use of music and décors. Such artificial conventions as the mask must be discarded. The dancer should use his expression to convey the emotions.

He postulated what he called *le ballet d'action,* in our language, the story ballet or the dance drama. He believed that the action should be obvious to the audience without the need of verbal explanation; some of his critics said that this was far from being the case in many of his own ballets. He used the analogy of language, to which I have already drawn attention. The letters of the alphabet are not enough, nor are words. It is necessary to form sentences and poems. Only then will ballet be a true branch of the theatrical art. His definition of ballet was 'the art of conveying our feelings and our passions to the spectator through the sincere expression of our movements, our gestures and our physiognomy'.

In spite of much opposition from the diehards accentuated by his aggressive temperament, his ideas prevailed. The leather mask was abandoned by the great dancers Vestris and Gardel – Noverre had written that, if only the men could show their emotions as delicately as the women, they would need no masks – and a new dimension entered into the dance. Other disciples carried his theories to Paris, London, Rome, Vienna and St Petersburg. It was one of his pupils, Dauberval, who produced the ballet *La Fille Mal Gardée,* the oldest ballet in the contemporary repertoire, though not always given with its original choreography.

Other choreographers working on similar lines were

the Italians, Angiolini and Vigano. Angiolini, who collaborated with Gluck, as had Noverre with *Alceste* in Vienna, in the production of the then revolutionary opera, *Orfeo,* believed that a ballet should move an audience to tears and not merely entertain. He looked back for inspiration to the ancient Roman pantomimes, or to what he imagined they had been. Vigano, nephew of Boccherini and a pupil of Dauberval, Noverre's pupil, did the choreography for Beethoven's only ballet, *Prometheus,* 1801. He went even further than Noverre and Angiolini, in the direction that Fokine was to take, telling his story in an expressive dance rather than in a combination of dance and mime. The work of these three men was not to be equalled until the full triumph of Russian ballet with the choreographic mastery of Michael Fokine.

The next of the founding fathers was the Italian, Carlo Blasis, a pupil of Vigano. He was an all-rounder in the Renaissance sense of the word; dancer, choreographer and teacher, art historian and writer on a variety of subjects that included economics. He travelled widely, sowing seeds in London, St Petersburg, Moscow and Paris. His headquarters were in Milan, where first he was principal dancer and then director of the ballet school. He codified the existing technique in two books, *Treatise on the Dance,* 1820, and *The Code of Terpsichore,* 1830; they are the basis of modern classroom technique. Through his museum studies he made many innovations, notably the *Attitude,* inspired by Gian Bologna's Mercury. He reaffirmed all that his great predecessor Noverre had said about the aesthetics of ballet.

The Birth of Ballet (Historical)

Many great names have been omitted from this record, all of artists who contributed to shape ballet as it is today. In an art that is not handed down in writing, though dance notation is making rapid strides today, tradition is all important. Every great dancer takes from this tradition and in his turn gives something to it. In Ulanova and Fonteyn there is an unbroken line of succession from Beauchamp and Noverre and their successors. It is simple to draw up the family tree and, as dancers are long lived, it can be done with very few names. One line goes from Noverre to Vigano, from Vigano to Blasis, to Lepri, to Cecchetti, who taught the Russians, Poles and our own Ninette de Valois, Marie Rambert, Ursula Moreton and others. This is an aristocratic art, even though it has become an art of the people.

3 : *The Romantic Movement*

Sunshine to Moonlight

BALLET by its very nature rapidly assimilates current trends in thought and, being an ephemeral art, rids itself of them equally quickly. The romantic movement was the great exception. Ballet after 1832 could never be the same again, the medium had found its ideal inspiration, and the results of that movement are still with us. Paradoxically it is from this romantic period that ballet dates its classicism.

Walter Scott, Heine, Schiller, Byron, Pushkin, Hugo, and especially Théophile Gautier, have all been assimilated into ballet. The great romantic composers and painters, on the other hand, made little contribution to the art, resulting in an imbalance that has yet to be fully remedied, a far cry from the Italian Renaissance and the days of *Le Roi Soleil*.

42

Among the many changes that romanticism brought with it, almost overnight, are the following: A completely new subject. Olympus and the Greek gods and heroes are banished. The scene is peopled by *wilis* from the German forests, sylphs from the highland moors, péris, dryads, naiads and ondines and, as an earthy foil, the smiling and buxom village maidens. The story has a fixed pattern: in the tragic works boy meets girl, boy wins girl, boy loses girl. There are three main characters; the hero, generally a cardboard figure, the heroine and the evil spirit who keeps them apart.

This change of story requires a change or rather an elimination of colour. It is no longer the bright sunshine of Greece or Rome, but the soft tree-filtered moonlight of shaded lakes, mountain streams and village graveyards. White predominates, hence the synonym for the romantic ballet, *le ballet blanc*. The ballerina's costume is of white tarlatan, making her as light and unsubstantial as a wisp of mist in a valley.

This suggestion of lightness, of a winged creature about to alight or to rise in flight or glide across a stream leads logically but, at the same time, imperceptibly to a startling new technical development, simultaneously a blessing and a curse. It is not known who was the first dancer to rise on to the tips of her toes, the points. It may have been Taglioni or the Russian, Avdotia Istomina, so highly praised by Pushkin.* The context demanded it and it happened, later to be aided and perfected by the strengthened point shoes, that were

* 'Istomina, the nimbly bounding
  With one foot resting *on its tip*
  Slow circling round its fellow swings
  And now she skips and now she springs' *Eugene Onegin.*

introduced in the early eighteen-sixties. Once discovered, the use of this extra inch of foot was to be used for dazzling feats of virtuosity as well as for romantic effect. It was to bedevil the art for so long that ballet was, by the beginning of the twentieth century, sometimes spoken of as *toe-dancing*. Noverre surely turned a *pirouette* in his grave.

Romanticism had yet another consequence, wholly bad. It led to such an idealisation of the ballerina that the male dancer, the original ballet dancer, no longer interested the choreographer or the public. He was only allowed to exist as a *porteur* or lifter and, at times, not even in that lowly capacity. As the century advanced he was replaced by a strapping woman, a principal-boy type, *en travesti,* with sometimes a delicate moustache sketched in.

This is how Castil Blaze, the historian of the Opéra describes the rapid decline of the male dancer: 'Our theatrical fashions have altered to such an extent that in 1832* the changes made in the personnel of the ballet were approved. The number of women dancers was greatly increased, the number of men decreased and those that remained lost a great deal of their importance. In 1846 the women dancers wore the tight trousers, the jackets and cloaks of the hussars and made a bold incursion into the male domain. No one in boxes or amphitheatre protested and the charming hussars in *Paquita* received the most gracious welcome.'

The whole dramatic balance and the physical orchestration had been upset, the essential *realism* had vanished. It has still to be fully restored outside of

---

* N.B. – The very year of *La Sylphide.*

44

Russia, though the public in the West is gradually beginning to accept the male dancer, especially when he is a Russian.

The first of these romantic ballets was *La Sylphide* 1832. It is still in the repertoire. It tells the charming story by Nourrit of a highlander, engaged to a village girl, who falls in love with a woodland sylph, winged and so light that she can float among the trees and look at the nestlings. A witch, whom the highlander had turned away when she came to him in the guise of a beggar, tells him that she can turn the sylph into a human, and weaves a magic scarf for the purpose. He gives the scarf to his beloved immortal, but her wings drop off and she dies. As he mourns by her body, the marriage procession of his fiancée and his friend passes by and he is left alone.

An ideal story for ballet, immortalised in the lithograph of the Highlander and the Sylph, it is a popular ballet in Denmark today, and has been revived in England by Marie Rambert. Had the music matched the subject it might have been as popular as *Giselle*. Taglioni as *La Sylphide* ushered in a new type of dancer, light and ethereal and of apparent fragility paving the way for Pavlova and Spessivtseva. It was to lend its name to Fokine's great neo-romantic *Les Sylphides*. But the most famous of all the romantic ballets was *Giselle*. Since its creation in 1841 it has never failed to fill theatres to capacity and to make or mar the reputation of a ballerina. It is worth discussing in a section of its own, since not only is it topical but it explains so many things about the nature of ballet.

Giselle

Giselle was conceived by the poet Théophile Gautier from an idea in Heine's *Lettres de l'Allemagne*, and made into a ballet by an experienced librettist, Saint Georges, with choreography by Coralli and Perrot, later revised by Petipa.

It treats of the familiar medieval legend that the dead seek to dance the living away with them to the grave, the subject of innumerable carvings and woodcuts. Only in this case the dead person is not a grinning, jerkily articulated skeleton, but a frail and beautiful girl who loved dancing with such passion that after death she was doomed to become a *wili*, a temptress who danced men to their doom. Certainly a promising subject and one in which dancing itself is the central theme.

But what are the reasons for its continued success? They go to the very heart of our subject. In the first place, the story fulfils Noverre's dictum of being easily intelligible. The central character requires not only virtuoso dancing but dramatic ability of a high order. Also, it is always fresh since there are a number of different ways in which it can be interpreted. The heroine is very much a real person with whom the audience can identify themselves. The hero is far less passive than the customary romantic *jeune premier,* and from Nijinsky to Nureyev successive male dancers have added a personality to the role. This hero is far from the standard hero when first we meet him. He is selfish, pleasure loving and a deceiver who keeps his rank and his previous betrothal a secret from the girl whose heart he has won. Nor is the villain, Hilarion, wholly black. When he is shown as such he is badly played and the whole work suffers. He is a man whose love is selfish. The role of Giselle combines the two great types of dancer I have mentioned, Sallé and Camargo, Taglioni and Elssler in one person. In the first act she is a peasant, earthy and human, a tremendous problem for a ballerina using a classical technique. And what a wide range of emotions this peasant girl must show from blissful happiness in a love that is returned, to disillusion, despair, insanity and death. In the second act she is a spirit, flitting and floating, darting and flying. But this, demanding as it is, still gives an incomplete picture of the role's vast scope. There is a strong dramatic link between Acts I and II, by no means always made apparent by the ballerina; in our day Pavlova, Spessivtseva, Markova, Ulanova and Chauviré have been supreme in this. In Act II Giselle is still the slave of her memories, her love has conquered death and she has to struggle against her nature as a *wili*, subject to her queen's demands, and her great love as a woman.

Gautier found a new dancer for this role, Carlotta Grisi, 'halfway between Taglioni and Elssler', and said of her that those who expected to see *entrechats* and *cabrioles* found their eyes dimmed by tears.

Few ballets can be interpreted or discussed at such depth. And *Giselle*, in spite of its 'romantic period' date, is truly romantic in spirit and therefore an ageless symbol of undying love.

This in itself is a sufficient reason for its survival out of so many ballets of the period. An additional reason is its music. And here we have another paradox. Adam's score, hastily written, is bad music from an absolute standard. It shocked Wagner. One could not listen to it in the concert hall save as a nostalgic reminder of the ballet itself; I cannot even hum it without seeing the incomparable Ulanova. Alone it is incomplete, but, taken in conjunction with the story and its simple and direct choreography, it is altogether admirable. In 1841 it was years ahead of its time in using *leit-motiv* to point the drama. Poet, composer and choreographer are working hand in hand, the indispensable formula for great ballet.

Not long after *Giselle,* ballet outside of Russia entered into a long period of decadence and near eclipse. Between *La Source* in 1866 and *Coppelia* in 1870, not a single ballet was produced at the Paris Opéra. *Coppelia* still holds the bill all over the world, partly through the delicate music of Delibes, so greatly admired by Tchaikovsky. In Swanilda it has the greatest of all roles for the soubrette. The male role of Franz was danced by a woman *en travesti* and this tradition was maintained at the Opera until recently. Delibes' *Sylvia,* produced in 1876, also survives, but with new choreography, in Paris by Lifar and in England by Ashton.

Enter the Russians

The romantic period was the dancer's golden age. The ballerina was the popular idol, and balletmasters produced ballet after ballet around the personality of the aetherial Taglioni, the eternal sylph, Elssler, 'the Spaniard from the North' – again the familiar contrast

Character Parts
6. Roland Petit as Cyrano de Bergerac (*Mike Davis*)
7. Vladimir Levashov as The God of the Forest (*L. Zhdanov*)

8. Margot Fonteyn in Act I, *Romeo and Juliet* (*Mike Davis*)

between the two types of dancer – Grisi, creator of *Giselle*, who to Gautier, enamoured of her, combined the two, Grahn, Cerrito, 'the dancing dragonfly', Dumilâtre and, in its heyday, the men, Jules Perrot and Lucien Petipa.

These ballets were produced to an almost computer-made formula, and soon bore as much relation to a vital art as the many keepsake annuals that were their exact contemporaries. Noverre had long been forgotten.

Deprived of the male dancer, ballet might well have died except as a music-hall entertainment, or as an interlude in a Grand Opera so welcome to the wealthy patron with his *petite amie* in the *corps de ballet*. This was the period when dancer's slippers are said to have taken the place of champagne glasses, when an entrée to *le foyer de la danse* was a sign of birth and wealth, and when the dancer's greatest contribution to art was the privilege that she shared with washerwomen and the acrobat of serving as a model for Monsieur Degas. Even that ardent *balletomane,* Théophile Gautier, who had created a masterpiece and also started the decadence, noted how the dancers ogled the boxes, chattered and giggled. This was in Paris which he was contrasting with St Petersburg where the ballet had held him enthralled.

Russia was to come to the rescue and to dominate the art for generations, so much so that today ballet all over the world pays tribute to Russian Ballet.

The reasons are many; political, economic, social and racial. The court dance was established in St Petersburg by Peter the Great as a deliberate step in his policy of Westernisation. It brought the women from their almost Eastern seclusion, it forced the men to abandon their ground-sweeping skirted coats and to adopt Western fashions. We have seen that from court to theatre is but a short step. In the reign of the Empress Anne a ballet school was opened, and soon there was a flourishing company that rivalled that of Paris, though until the beginning of this century the prestige and the high salaries belonged to the foreigners.

The particular form that ballet assumed and retains come from the nature of this vast country, part western, part oriental. Russia started with a rich and indigenous folk dance, varying greatly from province to province, in which the peasants expressed themselves naturally. Music and folklore were equally rich. The institution of serfdom, for all its inhumanity, brought one great benefit, it enriched the theatre. In addition to the companies supported by the Imperial Privy Purse, there were a large number of private companies owned by nobles and recruited from their peasants. This meant that at a time when ballet in the West was beginning to forget its origins and become decadent, in Russia it had close contact with the soil, it was a natural form of self-expression to its exponents and not just a means to an end. The great Catherine herself insisted on ballet being 'vraisemblable' and not an empty exercise in virtuosity, anticipating today's Soviet aesthetic. The Imperial Theatre recruited dancers from the private companies, thus preventing artistic inbreeding. Russia attracted all the great dancers and balletmasters from abroad, learnt from them, in particular from the Frenchman Duport, and when they stayed long enough, in its turn showed them fresh possibilities in dancing and especially in expressiveness. Already by 1812, time of the great patriotic war, when French dancers left in haste, one can talk of a ballet that is definitely Russian and, in Ivan Valberg, there is a Russian choreographer. The change was noted by the French on their return to St Petersburg.

The characteristics that are beginning to appear and that will be greatly developed are a new understanding of the principles of Noverre and a total identification of the dancer with his role. This can be seen in *Giselle*. Gautier himself calls it a suitable subject for a *pretty* ballet, he would certainly have been astonished at the depth given to his charming anecdote. The Russians from the time of their first *Giselle*, 1842, Anna Andreyanova, understood it as a drama. I hesitate to use the hackneyed phrase 'they gave it a soul', but the Russian word for soul, *dousha*, does convey my meaning; or, better still, they gave it the life that the puppet Petrouchka gains at the end of that great Russian dance drama, a valid symbol of their contribution.

Three foreigners played an outstanding role in the development of Russian ballet; Marius Petipa, from Marseilles, Christian Johanson, a Swede, and the Italian, Enrico Cecchetti. The name of Petipa is very much alive and his close partnership with Tchaikovsky has left us with the key works of our classical repertoire, as well as acting as an inspiration to modern choreographers. Petipa, active for nearly half a century, was a prolific worker – he composed thirteen four-act ballets, twelve three-act ballets, three two-act ballets, eighteen one-act ballets, as well as being responsible for seventeen revivals – and more of his works would have survived had their music been tolerable and their stories less contrived. As things were, most of the acts of his ballets would have been interchangeable without anyone noticing the difference.

The Sleeping Beauty and *Swan Lake** endure because their simple stories are true at any age. *Raymonda,* in spite of acceptable music by Glazounov, dates as much as *The Mysteries of Udolpho.*

This is the place to consider the hotly debated question of revivals and alterations.

The sentimental conservatism with which some critics assail so many revivals of the classics as differing from the original has no solid evidence to offer. Indeed, if one thing is certain, it is that no revival that anyone has seen is the same as the original. Moreover, it is doubtful if a replica of an original would be welcome today. Even in a younger and very familiar work, *Les Sylphides,* I have seen enormous differences over the years. Fokine, its creator, is known to have made seven versions. Choreography is not static, and the personality of the dancer who interprets the role inevitably leads to modifications, alterations and fresh traditions. The famous (I feel inclined to write 'notorious') thirty-two *fouettés* in the Black Swan Act of *Swan Lake,* for instance, were by no means always danced in Russia. The *prima ballerina assoluta* Kchessinska learnt the trick from the Italian, Legnani, and performed it sensationally, others substituted steps that they could perform with greater ease. Today these *fouettés* have become a commonplace, and they very rarely have a dramatic effect,

---

* Lev Ivanov working under Petipa was responsible for much of this.

unless the ballerina has a bad tumble. Whether to make completely new versions of these classics, as distinct from modifications, raises another and far more debatable point. It is then up to the new choreographer to succeed in the almost impossible challenge of competing, not merely with a familiar and long-accepted work, but also with our, perhaps exaggerated, memories of the first impact that it made on us. Can one imagine a new version of *Carmen*? As I write, I remember *Carmen Jones*. It had a certain vitality but I still stick to my point. I believe that these classics should be given new productions every decade, but are otherwise best left alone as far as the main pattern of the choreography is concerned. These ballets will be discussed at greater length later in the book.

Johanson, the next foreigner, brought the graceful French technique from his master, Bournonville. He excelled in teaching women, and was the master of one of the greatest generation of ballerinas the art has known.

Enrico Cecchetti, coming to St Petersburg with his compatriots Brianza, Zucchi and Legnani, added a fresh element, the strength and virtuosity of Italian technique, greatly modified through his contact with Russian dancers. He was the pupil of a pupil of Blasis.

The Russian school was now complete. It had gathered the best from all over the world, assimilated it and transformed it through the riches of its own vast physical and spiritual resources. The beginning of this century saw the complete triumph of Russian dancers on Russian stages; for a singer or a dancer to triumph at home is the ultimate accolade.

4 : *The Diaghilev Era*

I ENDED the last chapter by underlining the triumph of the Russian dancer, but this does not mean the final success of ballet as an art form. The Italian Virginia Zucchi moved such a sophisticated spectator as Alexandre Benois in a work, *Brahma,* that was tawdry nonsense from beginning to end. His constructive re-action was to argue, 'If she can move me in this rubbishy concoction, what a powerful thing is this art of dancing and how splendidly it could be used in the right hands'.

The *intelligentsia* had for the most part kept away from ballet, bored by the jingly music, the gorgeous but unimaginative sets and the formula choreography. Then there was the stranglehold tyranny of the points, tiptoe into and tiptoe out of every situation, however unsuited to the emotion, the place or the period. Isadora Duncan had shown the select few that it was possible to dance and interpret the music of masters, and, once again, the impressionable Benois was moved. Painter, writer and art historian, he was passionately concerned with introducing to Russia the exciting new painting from Paris, and ridding Russian painting of its didactic social story-telling. The slogan of the progressives of his day was 'art for art's sake'. He had surrounded himself with a brilliant group of young writers, musicians, painters and philosophers, who expressed themselves through a journal, The World of Art (*Mir Isskoustva*).

One of them was a newcomer, a young provincial, Sergei Pavlovitch Diaghilev. He was knowledgeable in the arts, though he practised none well. He was dynamic, self-opinionated, ruthless even, in following his aims, and master of subtle publicity. He was that rare thing, a dilettante of limited means, the very man needed to launch a new movement. When he was asked what he wanted to become, he replied, 'A Maecenas – with other people's money'. And that is exactly what he did become, and in doing so he gave ballet a new and glorious lease of life. The vein that he opened, when properly understood, is still far from exhausted.

At first Diaghilev's interests lay exclusively in painting and music. It was Benois who turned his attention to ballet and to the vast possibilities it could have in helping them to attain their artistic ends. Diaghilev later compared the ballet to fresco painting, where results not only can but must be obtained rapidly. The ballet scene was ripe for such outside help. Michael Fokine, a brilliant young choreographer, also an accomplished painter and musician, was finding his way blocked, in spite of Petipa's admiration, by the ultra-conservatism of the Maryinsky Theatre. He too had been impressed by Duncan, and believed that since the days of Noverre ballet had, with few brilliant exceptions, not made the most of its opportunities. He wanted to

55

enlist the help of the best artists, to eliminate sterile academism, and to see the roles of the arts that compose ballet revised in such a way that they become equal partners. His full aesthetic will be discussed in the appropriate place. With Diaghilev behind him, and with the aid of such painters as Benois and Bakst and such dancers as Karsavina and Nijinsky, Fokine succeeded in his aims, and in doing so revived ballet throughout Western Europe. His partnership with Stravinsky in *The Firebird* and *Petrouchka* was the most successful since that of Tchaikovsky and Petipa. Fokine's *Schéhérazade* with Bakst's inspired designs revolutionised stage décors and fashions, his *Le Spectre de la Rose,* danced by Nijinsky, raised the male dancer once again to the heights from which Gautier had toppled him. Within two years the word ballet meant *Russian* ballet, and this persisted for a quarter of a century. If it is not any longer so completely exclusive, it is still a mark of the highest distinction.

Diaghilev was not the man to rest on his laurels. He welcomed success, but at the same time it bored him. Also, he was a frustrated artist who created through others, educating them, challenging them, and goading them frantically to produce something new and arresting. He was terrified of stagnation, old age and death. He had not created Fokine or even discovered him; he had provided him with a wonderful opportunity. This was not enough for so restless an individualist, and after three years they parted. Diaghilev now launched a choreographer of his own in Nijinsky, his fabulous *premier danseur*. The result was *l'Après-midi d'un faune, Le Sacre du Printemps* and the beginning of a policy in which Diaghilev was to rejoice, that of shocking his public by anticipating their taste, and once they had accepted it, moving on again. Jeers, cheers and fisticuffs broke out at the première of the Faun. The cheers predominated and it was actually given an encore. The scandal had only begun. In a few days Paris was divided between the *faunistes* and the *anti-faunistes*. 'The public will never accept this animal realism,' wrote Calmette in the Figaro. Rodin leapt to its defence and was joined by such notables as Clemenceau, Briand, Poincaré, Anatole France, Barrès and others. Ballet had made its impact.

This shock policy was to last with but one nostalgic interlude for the rest of his life. When others have set out deliberately with such an aim it has failed. Diaghilev's success lay in his unique ability to mix what he called 'the ballet cocktail', gathering round him an artistic court not seen since *Le Roi Soleil*. He might well have said, '*Le ballet c'est moi*'.

Paris, after the Russian revolution, became his centre of inspiration, and he enlisted the help of such masters as Picasso, Derain, Braque, Matisse, Rouault, Tchelitchev, and others to design his sets, and commissioned scores from the leading composers of the day; Satie, Poulenc, Auric, Prokofiev. One source of strength of the Diaghilev ballet lay in the fact that, though Russian, it was never narrowly wedded to nationalistic themes, music or décors. Its inspiration was universal. He submitted his choreographers and dancers to a hot-house course of study in museums and archives. Jean Cocteau and Igor Stravinsky alone stood the pace, lasting the whole breathless journey and beyond.

57

I will select four works that illustrate Diaghilev's mastery as a mixer of cocktails: Massine's *Le Tricorne,* with its score by de Falla, costumes and décors by Picasso; Nijinska's *Les Biches,* score by Poulenc, décors and costumes by Marie Laurencin; the same choreographer's *Les Noces,* score by Stravinsky, costumes and décors by Gontcharova; and Balanchine's *Prodigal Son,* score by Prokofiev and costumes and décors by Rouault. Each one of these ballets is a whole because each one of the collaborators expresses the same emotion in his particular medium. Such perfect ballet-making no longer exists. It would be possible to change the décor of many of today's works, all too often improving them but without ever disturbing the balance. A brief exception to this sweeping but incontrovertible statement have been the ballets by Boris Kochno, Diaghilev's lieutenant of the last period, and of his 'pupil' in this field, Roland Petit, discoverer of Clavé and Carzou. Ballet today is ruled by the dancer-choreographer. It has been at its best in the hands of Molière, Gautier, Diaghilev, Cocteau and Kochno, non-dancers all.

I mentioned Diaghilev's one nostalgic interlude, it has proved of major importance to the history of ballet in Western Europe. In 1921, at the Alhambra in London, he produced Tchaikovsky's *Sleeping Beauty;* characteristically he called it *The Sleeping Princess,* claiming that there was no beauty available. This was an act of piety or nostalgia, produced on a St Petersburg scale with lavish sets and costumes by Bakst, and with an outstanding company of dancers, among them Olga Spessivtseva, for simplicity renamed Spessiva, Vera Trefilova, Ludmilla Schollar, Anatol Witzak, and Pierre

Vladimirov, the pride of the Maryinsky Theatre, who had never been seen in Western Europe.

The venture was a financial failure, it ran for three months while it should have run for a year to recoup its expenses. Diaghilev had so accustomed his public to the very latest that they could not accept this, to them, retrograde step, especially the music of Tchaikovsky. Yes, there was a period when Tchaikovsky was completely unacceptable, even though given the accolade by Stravinsky in a programme note. The full-length ballet failed, but it led to a popular one-act abbreviation, *Aurora's Wedding,* and also to a potted one-act *Swan Lake.* For the first time dancers, critics and the general public were introduced to the classical basis of ballet. In England this had a tremendous influence without which we might have lost our way and never have had a national ballet firmly based on a classical repertoire.

Parallel to Diaghilev were the activities of a ballerina of genius, Anna Pavlova. She showed to a large and uncritical public a sublime *Giselle,* potted versions of other classics, and her own inimitable dances in which, like Zucchi before her, she transformed the everyday into something miraculous. Apart from her those poignant poems, those monologue ballets, *The Dying Rose, La Valse Triste, the Dragonfly* and *The Dying Swan,* she excelled as no one has in moments of pure gaiety. Fokine considered that this more than anything revealed the true extent of her greatness since gaiety without triviality is the most difficult of all moods to express in action. Her famous Gavotte (Lincke), and that inspired fragment *Christmas,* (Tchaikovsky) which performed by anyone else might have descended to the bathos of a mass-produced greetings card, gave one a real experience of lightness not merely of body, but of spirit. Who in that famous *pas de deux* from *Don Quixote,* so often performed as a setpiece firework display, has ever shown such wit? That again is something different from gaiety. And still her wide range was not exhausted. The stirring *Bacchanal* was more truly Hellenistic in spirit than all the self-conscious attempts to evoke ancient rites that we have so often seen, sometimes with the Parthenon itself thrown in as a background. Her interpretation of oriental dance in *Ajanta Frescoes* led directly to the revival of the Hindu dance, moribund in its country of origin. Pavlova inspired audiences all over the world, many became dancers through her example. Ballet needed both Diaghilev and Pavlova to reveal itself to the full.

If her great public was uncritical, such enlightened writers as André Levinson saw in her example a corrective to many of Diaghilev's *épatiste* excesses. She surrounded herself by a large and well-trained company, as she herself often told me, 'no ballerina can stand alone', but somehow it always remained a solo performance. She fitted neither into the Imperial Russian Ballet nor in the Diaghilev ambiance, although in her early days both had destined her to their ballerina. But more of her when I deal with the aesthetics of ballet. Diaghilev and Pavlova together laid the foundations for the spread of ballet throughout the world.

Diaghilev died in 1929, Pavlova two years later. The further history of Russian ballet in exile, appropriately named *ballet russe* by the historian Prince Lieven, shows a steady decline, after a bright Indian summer under

Colonel de Basil, who with René Blum formed in Monte Carlo a company composed of the best elements in the Diaghilev Ballet, and of such brilliant newcomers as Irina Baronova, Tamara Toumanova, Tatiana Riabouchinska, André Eglevsky and David Lichine, all of them pupils of the ballerinas of St Petersburg's golden age, Trefilova, Egorova, Preobrajenska and Kchessinska, and in many ways closer to the great tradition than Diaghilev's later dancers. For a short time de Basil proved himself a strong and courageous impresario, and ballet owes him a lasting debt. He united the public of Diaghilev and Pavlova and increased it, taking ballet to three continents. His very success under the existing economic situation killed his enterprise. The dancers, worn out by constant travel, were tempted by outside offers, there were splits and rivalries, and once the connection with Monte Carlo had been broken, there was never the time for stock-taking or creation. A train, even an American drawing-room car, is a poor substitute for the Hotel de Paris, a drug store is less inspiring than a café. The Diaghilev inheritance had been squandered, *ballet russe* was a thing of the past.

5 : *National Ballet*

WE have seen that ballet from its origins had catered for an élite, in its earliest days an aristocratic élite, in Diaghilev's time an intellectual élite. Scarcely a memoir of his period fails to mention the impact of his ballet on all the arts. All the French critics saw the great Paris Exhibition of Arts Decoratifs as a summing-up of and a monument to an achievement that had altered the eye of the civilised world.

We now come to an era of popularisation, ballet for everyman. The large travelling company had its vast public, but it was no longer viable either financially or creatively. Also, once the large company had become completely international and had no true roots for its sustenance, it withered and died. Only a truly national expression of any art can really become of international importance.

Once more ballet returns to the opera house, where it was originally nurtured, cradled in a permanent home and supported by state subsidies. And it is here that the Diaghilev inheritance has been put to its greatest use.

His alumni have given ballet permanence. Serge Lifar went to the Paris Opéra, revived the glorious traditions of that house and created a generation of dancers who lived for their art and not merely for the pleasure and rewards of *le foyer de la danse*. France, once again after an interval of nearly half a century, produced a *prima ballerina assoluta,* in Yvette Chauviré. The Opéra too fathered its inspired rebels in Roland Petit and Renée Jeanmaire. They were to spread the French influence abroad after Lifar's possibly too absolute authority. Not the least of the benefits of an Academy is to produce rebels. c.f. Petipa and Fokine.

George Balanchine was to plant the ballet tradition firmly in the United States, where previously it had been suspect with the intellectuals as something foreign and frivolous. Frivolous it certainly was, when one remembers a performance of *Schéhérazade* with elephants on the bill; this did not refer to the dancers. His path was a difficult one, in spite of the help of the fanatical Lincoln Kirstein, and only recently has he, through the substantial support of the Ford Foundation, found the security essential to permanence and development.

In England two other Diaghilev alumni* planted the seed of national ballet: Marie Rambert with her flair for discovery, and Ninette de Valois with her genius for long-term planning that resulted in the Royal Ballet with its two companies and its Royal School.

Germany has abandoned its modern dance, called by the young 'the old-fashioned dance that mother used to enjoy', and ballet companies are attached to all its many

* I am told that Peter Ustinov calls them 'wearers of the old school tights'.

63

opera houses, the talent spread out too thin at present to make an international impact, though once again Noverre's Stuttgart, now controlled by John Cranko, seems to point the way. Inspired by the English example, Australia, South Africa and Canada have their own companies, and there is a flourishing state company in Turkey under the direct guidance of the inspired and inspiring Ninette de Valois. And so this pattern of nationalism in ballet continues.

And once again Russian Ballet as distinct from *ballet russe* comes to the fore, its dancers an exciting revelation, products of a great tradition that has been continually enriched by the national genius for dancing, by the increased opportunities given it by the Soviet government and by an eager new public. There are some thirty companies and eighteen schools throughout the length and breadth of Russia, Uzbeks and Siberians, Tadjeks and Georgians, all are making their contribution. In Russia it is still taken more seriously as a branch of theatre than in any other country.

There has been a succession of great ballerinas to continue the path traced by Kchessinska, Preobrajenska, Pavlova, Karsavina, Spessivtseva. Semenova, Dudinskaya and Ulanova already belong to history, and are passing on their knowledge. Such knowledge, handed down directly by great exponents, constitutes the greatest strength in Soviet ballet as it did in French ballet in the days of Noverre. Plisetskaya, Struchkova, Kondratieva are in full bloom, Maximova, Sizova, Besmertnova follow in their footsteps, and Vladimir Vassiliev is surely one of the greatest males dancers that even Russia has produced.

Swan Lake
9. Maia Plisetskaya as Odette (U.S.S.R.)
10. Maia Plisetskaya as Odile (*M. Murazov*)

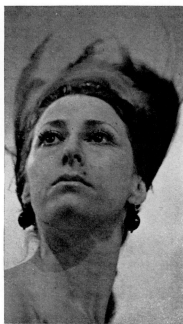

11. Primitive dancers – African Ballet (*Mike Davis*)

At the beginning there was a French and Italian *school*, then a Russian *school*. Now there are English and American *schools* clearly recognisable, capable of influencing one another through the exchange of visits, artists and ideas.

Part II

6 : *What is Ballet?*

A Definition

I HAVE now attempted a partial answer to the question *What is a Ballet?* by putting it into the general context of history, geography and economics and outlining, just sufficiently for my purpose, its story in time and space. Many of its guiding principles will already have emerged from what I have written. In this section I will try to analyse it as logically as possible, always allowing for the fact that if, as Gautier said, 'it is difficult to write for feet', it is almost as difficult to write of a kinetic visual art without being able to use quotations in the same way as the music and dramatic critic. To write of the dance is an attempt to go back into time and to make the ephemeral eternal, to draw the attention to something exciting that is no longer there.

Ballet is a combination of the arts of dancing, poetry, music and painting. The dancers are trained in the school of classical ballet as developed by the great dancing masters from the time of Beauchamps onwards. The theme or story is told, or, in a non-dramatic ballet, the atmosphere indicated, by the choreographer who 'orchestrates' a group of dancers who are guided in rhythm and expression by the music, and who dance in costumes and against a setting devised for the purpose. Choreographer, dramatist or poet, composer and decorative artist, work as a team, each one expressing the same idea in his own medium.

Here then is the dry bare statement that I shall analyse and illustrate both from the point of view of the ballet-makers and their audience.

The Dancer as an Instrument

There are two aspects to the dancer; he is a musical instrument and the player on that instrument; André Levinson called the unforgettable Vera Trefilova 'a dancing Stradivarius'.

The dancer is selected in the first place purely for his potential as an instrument. Has he the physique that will respond to and develop through the training? Selection must take place between the ages of ten and eleven. Making the instrument is a gradual process, lasting from eight to nine years, but training the perfected instrument continues throughout the dancer's career.

The physique required by the male is a slim, straight and supple body, a height of not less than 5 feet 8 inches, straight knees and legs, a supple and well-shaped foot with a well-arched instep, and a handsome appearance. The exceptional great dancer can triumph over physique, giving, through command of the stage, an impression of height. Nijinsky, Babillé, Nureyev, are all of medium stature. The female needs a straight spine, suppleness, a not too big head well set on well shaped shoulders, straight legs that can be rotated from the hips, straight knees, a well-arched instep, and toes that can be a suitable platform for point work. A height of between 5 feet 4 inches and 5 feet 7 inches, and, again, good looks. By good looks I do not mean beauty queen looks so much as a face that can, with the aid of make-up, appear attractive to the audience. There is such a thing as a ballet face and certain physical types that repeat themselves. A famous St Petersburg *balletomane,* General Bezobrazov, said, 'Show me her face and I will tell you whether she can dance'. Experts will testify that this is not as absurd as it would seem. Few potential dancers have the perfect physique; training can correct certain defects, intelligence and exceptional ability can mask others, at times turning them to positive advantage. The good teacher has a flair for anatomy, and in the great state training schools orthopaedists, assisted by X-rays, are continually called on for advice.

There are types of dancer just as among singers, there are bassos, baritones and tenors. There are the rare classical dancers from whom the ballerinas are chosen. They interpret ethereal roles and must conform to the highest ideal of physique. The character dancer, the balletic peasant, requires a sturdier type. The *demi-caractère* dancer, our mezzo-soprano, comes in between the two; maid of all work, she will be called upon at the wave of a baton to be an enchanted swan or a Spanish villager. Some ballerinas may also excel in character roles, the reverse is never the case. The essence of the training is its gradual build up. The first period is taken up with the correct placing of the body, and there can be no shorts cuts. A dancer spoilt in the early years is often a dancer spoilt for good.

I have already mentioned the technique of dancing from an historical point of view. Its assimilation requires a good memory, perfect co-ordination and quick thinking. Without this type of intelligence no instrument can be put to work.

Finally it is tempting to discuss the dance from the point of view of nationality but difficult to go beyond generalisations, especially when discussing racial characteristics. Both British ballet and Russian ballet draw on so many races for their dancers. In comparing British and Russian dancers one could say that one big difference lies in the greater maturity of the Russian dancer and in the fact that folk dancing is a part of the Russian environment. The English dancer tends to be reserved and lyrical, the Russian more expansive and more naturally at home in the medium. As Levinson wrote, 'The rigorous artifices and measured graces of western ballet were saturated with slavonic sensibility with its melodious melancholy and its tumultuous lyricism'.

The Dancer as an Artist

The preceding section deals with an aspect of the dancer that the audience rightly takes for granted. Selection has been made, a rigorous selection over many years; only about ten per cent of those in serious professional training pass through the sieve as the work becomes more and more complex.

But it is the finished article that the audience is watching and therefore I am going from now on to deal with the dancer from the spectator's point of view. What exactly can the dancer communicate and at how many different levels?

The lowest level is a purely mechanical achievement, that of a great difficulty overcome, the solution of a problem in dynamics. When a dancer turns once, the effect is negligible, but multiply that by thirty-two and it becomes a feat. It may be out of context, it may even jar from the point of view of dramatic logic, but it receives applause as acrobatics or as a sporting achievement. This reaction to the sporting achievement is very noticeable on the rare occasions when a dancer tumbles and is applauded on picking himself up far more than if he* had never fallen. In some ballets, notably *Swan Lake,* that very applause rudely suspends the magic. On rare occasions, such feats, danced by exceptional ballerinas, have a magic of their own, and the excitement generated belongs to the ballet as a whole; this becomes *coloratura* dancing. Maia Plisetskaya is today's supreme example of the *coloratura* dancer following the path traced by La Camargo.

There is therefore a very definite distinction to be made between mechanics and technique. True technique is directed to an end, to the expression of an emotion intended by the choreographer. Mechanics produce an emotion for their own sake.

It is not necessary for the spectator to know the

* It is more often *she* who falls, but I use the masculine when speaking of dancers in general. They have been ignored too long.

technique of dancing in order to enjoy or to understand ballet. It can be a positive disadvantage to name each step and thereby lose sight of the poetry. It is often an uncomfortable experience to watch a performance in the company of an obviously technically conscious dancer. Kicks and nudges apart, the remarks, approbatory or otherwise, are a distraction. Call a performer a 'technical dancer' and you damn him, since the essence of any art is to conceal technique.

The essential quality is grace, that is phrasing, fluidity, harmony, the making of words into a poetic whole. All of which is bound up with the dancer's re-action to music, and it goes far deeper than a purely rhythmic reaction, than what one might call the 'primitive tom-tom reaction'. The truly musical dancer is born not made, and is always the exception. The vast majority are *made* dancers, competent artisans rather than artists. In every field the word *artist* is abused these days, craftsman in itself is a proud title. As Valéry said of the sublime dancer in *L'Ame et la Danse, 'la musique lui change son âme'.*

Les Sylphides is a supreme test of the dancer's musicality. It is totally devoid of meaning when the dancer does not feel the music of Chopin. This is what the art of dancing can do; make music visual by trans-forming it into movement. There is, as Diaghilev so often said, no *corps de ballet* in *Les Sylphides,* every dancer must be an artist. There is no plot or characterisation to hide behind – this is rightly called *a romantic reverie* – hence the rarity of a perfect performance. Many a famous ballerina has failed here. Fokine's *Carnaval* presents even greater difficulties, since the

71

music depicts such a variety of subtle characters, not one of whom can be interpreted by reason alone. Frederick Ashton's *Symphonic Variations* (César Franck) and Balanchine's *Sérénade* (Tchaikovsky) are other test pieces of musical interpretation in which the music and the music alone constitutes the libretto.*

But the complete dancer requires further attributes, all, however, closely linked to the music, though less obviously than in the examples that I have quoted. The ballerina and the premier danseur must have dramatic ability of a high order. This presents itself differently in the classical and modern dramatic ballets.

In the classical ballets the characters tend to be *flat;* a succession of noble princes and the loving and beautiful trapped heroines of fairy tale and legend. The steps are clearly indicated with almost mathematical precision, but the interpretation belongs to the dancer, who has greater opportunities to be creative than in any other ballets. Another paradox; the most severely technical classical works allow the greatest freedom for individuality and self-expression. Hence their enduring quality.

I saw this vividly illustrated at the Bulgarian Varna Dance Competitions, 1964, where it was possible to see a dozen interpretations of the same classical ballets in one evening, danced by young ballerinas from a dozen different countries. The steps were the same, but in each case we saw something entirely fresh, more exactly a creation rather than an interpretation. The role is built up of countless small details that add up to the whole.

*Hence my active dislike of the term 'abstract' to describe such works.

72

Let us take a familiar example, *Swan Lake*. Here the ballerina has two roles, the heroine Odette, sensitive, loving, bewildered, pathetic and Odile, her brilliant, self-assured and evil double and rival. It is rare to find the perfect Odette and Odile in one dancer. But in each role itself there are infinite opportunities. For instance, some dancers suggest that for all Odette's pathos, she is a princess, proud and protective of the other enchanted swan-maidens by whom she is surrounded. Some stress the swan aspect, others her human nature. Odile must be made plausible and not shown merely as a brilliant ballerina performing circus tricks. Her triumph is in winning the prince's allegiance from Odette and not in having performed thirty-two *fouettés*.

The role of the little princess Aurora in *The Sleeping Beauty* requires even more filling in, without it the famous Rose *adagio* with four cavaliers is not a dance in which the sixteen-year-old Aurora is choosing a suitor but a brilliant and unrelated *divertissement*. Watch Margot Fonteyn in the role, and the whole stage is drawn into the action, beginning with her father and mother with whom, like a loving daughter, she is constantly *en rapport*. The finger-pricking episode becomes something positive, a miniature drama of Giselle quality, as this cosseted darling, who has never been crossed, felt pain or heard an angry word, suddenly realises she has been hurt, can scarcely believe it, turns to her parents for reassurance and finally sinks into a merciful sleep. Too often this is merely something negative and we can feel no sympathy or possible identification with the role, though we may enjoy beauty of line for its own sake, which some misguided super-sophisticates find sufficient. And this acting must be positive from everyone on the stage. Something intensely dramatic has happened. Everyone must react strongly if we, in the audience, are to react. It is this total acting that is the supreme strength and quality of Russian Ballet, where Stanislavsky has made such an important contribution to the art.

The role of the male cavalier is still more difficult to fill. First there is the purely dancing aspect, the behaviour of the cavalier in any *pas de deux*. He must continually convey to the audience 'isn't she beautiful? Isn't she light? Look at her, how privileged I am'. The gallant cavalier can double the effect of his ballerina not only physically, that is obvious, but also psychologically. This attitude of the male dancer is basic and positive quite apart from the dramatic context. He must be far more than a *feed* or a *stooge,* and there is so little room in which to manoeuvre. Nijinsky and the dancers that followed him built up the role of Albrecht in *Giselle.* The material was implicit in the libretto since the prince is first seen as an aristocratic philanderer who is shocked into a repentance that grows into true love.

What of these colourless princes in *Swan Lake* and *The Sleeping Beauty*? Rudolph Nureyev has shown that they can be given character in plenty. His boredom and lack of purpose in *Swan Lake,* before his great adventure begins, establishes a very positive personality that he later develops. This is not acting in a vacuum, his relationship to his mother and the court followers is very clearly indicated.

There is another side to acting in the classics. In the original productions the situations were shown in mime, a fixed formula of gesture; hand on heart – I love you. Superbly done by a Karsavina this could be meaningful. Moreover, these gestures have a natural origin as one can see if one watches a group of Italians seated round a café table. In modern ballet it has ceased to exist, and the tendency has been in the classics especially in the Soviet Union, to replace the mime by expressive or *recitative* dancing. This change has been hotly debated. There is much to be said on either side. My own view is that the dancer of today is out of sympathy with mime, but that were it done sparingly, with conviction and imaginatively, the audience would react as is proved by the tiny sample in *La Fille Mal Gardée*. On the whole, however, one must agree with the logic of Fokine; it is more effective for the dancer just to make his entrance without underlining it with mime, 'I have come here'.

Acting in the modern balletic drama is on a different basis. The role is more positively conceived by the choreographer, and we in the audience accept it more readily because we have no preconceived ideas. It is a commonplace that no experienced dancer can fail in a role that he has created. In those revealing Varna contests it was noticeable that in later stages of the contest, where dancers could choose their own roles from the contemporary repertoire, all of them gained far higher marks than in the classical qualifying rounds.

We have seen then that balletic acting of any kind is not dumb acting, television with the sound turned off, but an absolute. In the classics it is a complete expression of the dancer's personality and, in modern works, of the dancer and choreographer in a closer

75

contact. This problem of balletic acting will be met with once more in the section on the librettist's role.

A dancer who is musician and actor combined is a rarity, but there is a still higher plane seen but once or twice in a generation. Such a dancer transports us to the mystic origins of the art. This occurs when the dancer, by a process of complete identification, surrenders herself – I use the feminine here because my examples are ballerinas – so completely to her role that she can convey a moving experience to her audience, can convey a reality not through the brain but direct to the emotions. Then the role becomes more than the character of a heroine, it is a statement about life itself. And the dancer herself can echo the words of the sculptor of the Temple of Elura, 'Oh, how did I make it?'.

My three examples are from performances by three great Russian ballerinas.

The first is Tamara Karsavina in *Le Spectre de la Rose*.

This is a *pas de deux* but never the less a complete ballet by Fokine set to Weber's *Invitation à la valse*. It was conceived by the poet Jean Louis Vaudoyer and based on four lines of a poem by Théophile Gautier, in the way that Gautier himself had found inspiration from Heine. Vaudoyer modestly described his role as introducing Fokine to Gautier. It was a felicitious introduction as Gautier greatly admired Weber. It shows a young girl, in the original, Karsavina, who has just returned from her first ball. She comes through the French windows of a bedroom, flooded by moonlight, clutching a red rose that an admirer has given her. She is happily tired and sinks into a chair to dream. Her dream conjures up the spirit of the rose, in the original, Nijinsky. He dances with her in a transcendental version of her ballroom dance. She floats as one does in a dream. Dawn is breaking, the dream is ending and the spirit of the rose makes a spectacular leap, out of the window and her experience. She awakens, and in that awakening comes the moment of truth. It is the truth about adolescence, an unforgettable experience in thirty seconds of magic. She had gone to sleep a child and awoken a woman.

My second example by the same choreographer is more striking because it comes about through material that has become so hackneyed. It is that ballet monologue, *La Mort du Cygne,* as danced by Pavlova to the music of Saint-Saëns. Ballet is an ephemeral art, and this ballet, which is about the solitude of death, is a poem to the ephemeral. The proud graceful swan dances, agonises and is no more. The cessation from exquisite movement to nothingness, the essence of this poem, was made positive by Pavlova alone. It is now a concert piece, barely tolerable to those who experienced the original. Ulanova alone attempted to give it a new meaning, the glory and heroism that triumphs over death, leaving something positive behind. It is Pavlova's interpretation that survives.

The third example is that of Galina Ulanova in Lavrovsky's *Romeo and Juliet* to music by Prokofiev. We see Juliet the spoilt child romping with her nurse. Suddenly she catches sight of herself in the mirror and notices her swelling breasts. She is proud and happy, but there is also apprehension at the loss of the security of childhood. This adolescent experience is the prelude to tragedy.

77

These three great Russians have given *Giselle* a meaning that transcended the work itself. Ulanova, like Valéry's Athikté, 'was not acting the role of a lover ... no mime, no theatre. No, no! Nothing fictitious. Why pretend, my friends, when one has movement and rhythm, which are the reality within reality ... She was the incarnation of love itself.'

No other medium could convey so clearly and in such an instant of time so vivid a truth. There could be other examples. Alas, not many. Sometimes a young dancer, glorying in a new-found liberty given by a mastery of technique, will convey, for a performance or two, such an impression before this feeling has become a common-place, and routine and a conscious discipline draw the veil between role and reality.

It is for such moments as these that the *balletomane* sees the familiar works night after night, hoping for theatre alchemy. Can we ever explain or analyse such art? Isn't reason, as Valéry's Éryximaque says in *l'Ame et la Danse,* 'sometimes the faculty that makes us understand nothing about our body?'

7 : *The Choreographer*

THE word *choreographer* originally meant a writer of dances. Today it has come to mean the actual author of the movements. Serge Lifar has suggested, rightly, I feel, that *choréauthor* would be the more explicit word.

There is general agreement as to what makes a good dancer; the great dancer is instantly recognised by public and critic alike. Once again from the Varna experience it was shown that in the case of outstanding dancers the marks of eighteen judges of different ages, countries and experience were almost identical. And the applause of a not-too-experienced public echoed their verdict. On the subject of choreography, tastes and opinions differ widely. However, in spite of the fact that judgment here is far more subjective, there are a few basic laws that can and must be formulated.

Today everything danced is called choreography. We must make an immediate distinction between dance arrangement, which is the stringing together of class-room steps from the classical repertoire – 'Balbus built a wall' – and something truly creative.

Clearly the first, in a sense the only, rule is that *the impression to be communicated must be communicated better through the medium of the dance than in any other art form,* otherwise the whole exercise is a waste of time and effort.

We immediately come up against plays that have been transformed into ballet; two very special cases being Lavrovsky's *Romeo and Juliet,* already quoted, and Helpmann's *Hamlet.* Are these merely illustrations for the illiterate? Do they transgress this first rule? I believe not, although they could not exist without the plays that inspired them, but then Shakespeare's plays themselves owe their origin to previous works. Lavrovsky has attempted a genuine translation of verbal poetry into the poetry of movement and, at moments, the parallelism is inspired. There are moments too, like the one I have quoted, where an aspect of a character is shown in sharp relief. This is translation, but on a very high level – that rare case where the translation of a poem is itself a work of art. Clearly poetry is more suitable for translation into ballet than is prose.

Helpmann's *Hamlet* is not a translation but a commentary on the play, using Freudian analysis in a poetical manner. It is not so much the story as a development of the words – 'Perchance to dream'. It is in one sense less complete than Lavrovsky's work, since in order to understand it, it is essential to know one's *Hamlet.* In this case Helpmann was not asking too much in expecting such knowledge from his audience, but both these ballets are exceptions, and the rule stands.

Another basic rule is that the choreographer must translate natural movement and natural indications of

12. Ekaterina Maximova and Vladimir Vasiliev in *The Stone Flower* (*L. Zhdanov*)

13. Natalia Bessmertnova in *Giselle* (*V. Bliokh*)

expression into dance form. When he is too naturalistic, he fails because naturalism is not at home on the stage and quarrels with theatre conventions. When he is too remote from nature, he cannot touch his audience, and ballet becomes a mere decoration. He must, if the ballet has a narrative, aim at realism within the accepted convention. This sounds too obvious for comment; it is, in fact, at times more obvious to the audience than to the choreographer.

Let me give some examples of this lack of *realism*. In pre-Fokine times, if a ballerina was famed for a pseudo-Spanish or Hungarian dance, she would perform it on the slightest pretext, even if the scene were set in Poland. Prince Wolkonsky, a reforming director of the Imperial Theatres, quotes one terrifying example, a smirking chorus dancing *sur les pointes* on Wagner's Venusberg. Fokine's first brush with reaction was when he discarded point shoes for a ballet with a Greek setting. He was told by a director with an R.S.M. mentality, 'You teach the classic dance and wish to present your pupils in some totally different form of art. You will please postpone this until some future date, and now compose a ballet in the customary style.' The points would only have been justified in a highly stylised work as, for instance, in a play set on Olympus that uses a modern idiom.

Two further examples are more subtle, of the type that disconcerts an audience without the audience always knowing the exact reason.

In one case a table was being used as a gate, and the dancers could only enter a garden by moving the table to one side. This was clearly established, and then for

F

no reason at all the table was never used in that way again and the dancers passed around it, evidently walking through what we had been led to believe was a hedge or a fence.

In my other example, the dancers clearly established that there was a stream in the middle of the stage, women washed their clothing there and splashed one another. And then, suddenly, this was forgotten and they walked and danced in it. If they did not feel wet, we did.

The choreographer must be consistent and everything within the particular convention must be plausible. Illusions are easily shattered.

The choreographer may, and indeed must, depart from the basic classroom technique. His very vocation may well originate from the need to revolt against this discipline; a choreographer's early works are often expressed in terms of his own physical needs. Fokine once complained that some dancers were so turned out that they had forgotten how to walk normally. But though the choreographer can make the greatest demands on his dancers, he must always bear in mind that they are human beings and not machines. It is one of the most common faults today for a choreographer in a feverish search for originality to give his dancers awkward and even dangerous lifts to perform. If the dancers find them uncomfortable to perform, it is quite certain that the spectators find them uncomfortable to watch. Moreover many of these strained movements produce a suspension of belief, since they are out of context and attract attention to themselves for their own sake. When in a painting the hands, for instance, focus the attention at the expense of the whole, the painting is a failure, however ingeniously those hands are painted. Moreover, where dancing is concerned, the awkward movement usually interferes with the flow of the music. I can think of more than one ballet where certain movements are made so complex that only one performance in half a dozen, and I am writing of highly trained dancers, runs smoothly. The audience must feel that, granted the situation, the action is inevitable.

Good choreography must be good theatre. This excludes padding and repetition, often the fault of the composer, but the choreographer, when working with a living composer, must be clear in his mind what it is that he requires.

Good choreography must always be governed by the same rules of composition as painting and sculpture, bearing in mind the relation of foreground and background, and the effect of colour as well as line. His problems of composition are more complex than those of the painter, since he is not only concerned with the static. He is, in fact, composing hundreds of paintings, and his static groups are the resolution of climax of these many paintings.

Dame Ninette de Valois' *Rake's Progress* is an admirable example. Her inspiration came from Hogarth's narrative paintings. It is comparatively easy to reproduce these on the stage, but about as futile as a series of *tableaux vivants*. Her problem was to 'paint' hundreds of pictures in such a way that, if movement were suspended at any one moment, the result would be a painting in the Hogarth manner. To take particular paintings as an inspiration, that is to translate one visual art into another, is rarely successful. Dame Ninette succeeded to perfection, both in this work and in her Rowlandson ballet, *The Prospect Before Us*. She did not succeed in an early work inspired by Manet's *Bar aux Folies-Bergères*. Impressionism does not lend itself to balletic translation. The many Degas-inspired ballets have all failed and have become merely whimsical.

To set in motion once again a moment that interested the painter for reasons totally unconnected with the dance does not make sense.

I mentioned the choreographer's concern with colour. It is for him to indicate to the designers how he is going to use his dancers so that the colours can be blended harmoniously. The good choreographer, therefore, must be familiar with the great museums and art galleries. Noverre, Blasis and Fokine are all in agreement on that point.

The greatest problem in ballet today, as always, is to find choreographers. They are scarcer by far than either purely creative or interpretative artists, not because they are greater, but because of the nature of their work that lies somewhere between that of the playwright and the producer, though the parallel must not be pushed too far. It is indeed 'difficult to write for the feet'. In twenty years of absolute rule Diaghilev only used a half dozen. Of these, Fokine was already fully developed, Nijinsky only really succeeded with one ballet, *l'Après midi d'un faune,* Balanchine had already started in Russia, Lifar only had time to produce one ballet for him, *Le Renard*. His only real creation was Leonide Massine, whom he trained from adolescence. He developed an already mature Nijinska. This then is the record of ballet's greatest animator. And everywhere it is the same. In the whole world there are only a handful of choreographers.

The reason is obvious from what has gone before. The nature of the work is creative but dependent. The artist's paints or his clay are human beings with a physique that sets narrow limits to their plastic possibilities, and who have a personality and will of their own. 'Even the most talented dancers,' writes Fokine, 'have their favourite movements and transplant them from ballet to ballet'.

Some choreographers work in very close collaboration with their dancers, and are inspired by a particular dancer. This can produce brilliant results, as in the case of Roland Petit's *Carmen* with Renée Jeanmaire. This means, however, that no revival with a change of cast is ever totally satisfactory. Other choreographers come to the first rehearsal with a set plan, as if they were producing an already written play. Ballet needs both kinds.

In addition to the problem of working in the medium of human beings, the choreographer is severely limited in his expression by the music. The great choreographers have a conductor's knowledge of music. Fokine would take a score to bed with him and read it like a novel. Balanchine has passed through the conservatoire and is an accomplished pianist. The early choreographers were always musicians.

I have already underlined the choreographer's relationship to painting and sculpture. In addition it is necessary for him to be a producer who can explain to his dancers what it is all about. Fokine, rehearsing *Petrouchka*, danced and mimed every role from principal's to walkers' on. Too many choreographers demonstrate the steps and keep the cast in the dark as to their significance.

Ideally the choreographer, who must be a competent dancer, should also have passed through an art school, a dramatic academy and a conservatoire of music. It is for this reason that the classical ballet must be the foundation of every repertoire, an education, a discipline and an inspiration.

8 : *The Role of the Librettist*

WRITING ballet stories is deceptively complex. The French and the Russians have excelled at it, each in a different direction. It has, as yet, not been sufficiently studied in this country.

It has often been said that the libretto of any ballet could be written on the back of an envelope. This is true, with the proviso that the smaller the envelope the better the ballet.

The medium has stringent rules that are all too frequently broken. Much ballet is completely unintelligible without copious programme notes. Conversely, the programme notes of a perfect ballet often have very little meaning without the action and the music.

The dramatist's limiting factor is that he can only depict action in the present tense. If he wants to delve into the past, he can only do so by a flashback. Many of the simplest concepts cannot be communicated without words: 'She is my sister-in-law', 'This time last year'. Only comparatively direct emotions may be shown; love, hatred, anger, greed, fear, pride, jealousy, awe, grief, hesitation, suspicion. None of the complex psychology of an Ibsen or a Tchekov. No mixed motives. The characters tend to be black or white; there is only the possibility of very few touches of grey that an exceptional artist can convey.

This severe discipline would seem to rule out ballet completely as a serious dramatic art. It does not, any more than the still more severe disciplines imposed on the Byzantine artist, rule out the communication of a profound religious sentiment. For every ten thousand formula eikons, mass-produced, a handful arrived, through this discipline, at complete communication. Where there is no discipline and it is go as you please, you have the breakdown in communication that exists in so much contemporary art.

The ballet dramatist, dealing in symbols, has a very wide field. He need not tell a story at all, but merely suggest an atmosphere. *Les Sylphides,* the very essence of romanticism without the claptrap and the property figures of the romantic period. Moonlight, a poet and the sylphs he has conjured up. He may take a theme, youth and adolescence *Le Spectre de la rose,* or ephemerality and the loneliness of death, *The Dying Swan.* He can tell a story that has a number of possible shades of meaning. *Petrouchka* is the supreme example of this.

A showman musician brings his puppets to the fair in the Admiralty Square at St Petersburg. They are, Petrouchka, in legend the equivalent of our Punch, but shown here as a pathetic figure of fun, 'he who gets slapped', the ballerina, pretty, pert and heartless and the Blackamoor, primitive, superstitious and lecherous.

Petrouchka loves the ballerina who flirts with him, leads him on and then turns her attention to the Blackamoor. Petrouchka is heartbroken when he finds the pair together. There is an affray and Petrouchka is killed by the Blackamoor.

The holiday crowd is frightened by the realism of the scene. The police are called, but the magician soon reassures them. Petrouchka is only a rag doll whom he drags off, limp and dangling. It is all an illusion. But is it? As the crowd withdraws he leaves the scene dragging the sawdust doll behind him. Then he hears a noise and looks back. There is Petrouchka gesticulating from the top of the booth; a few despairing movements and he collapses. He is dead, but he has lived.

That is the straightforward narrative, enjoyable in itself with all the colour and excitement of the fair and the vivid life of the crowd, not a *corps de ballet* but living people, every one of them, from the nursemaids, the coachmen, the merchants, the gipsies, the street dancers and the revellers to the small student.

When we take a closer look at this colourful ballet it gains in depth and there are a rich variety of possible meanings. There is the power for evil in the man who gains control over the minds and bodies of others. There is the character of Petrouchka himself, a typical Russian conception, the man with a soul who is struggling to find himself, the 'idiot' too sensitive for his surroundings. He could be from the Marxist point of view seen as an exploited moujik. He could be viewed from the Christian point of view as the martyr who lost his life and saved his soul or from the Freudian angle of the man who found his *ego*. The contrasting characters are those people who, swayed by their desires and without guiding principles, are no better than automata, the Freudian concept of those guided by the Id. It may show that a brave revolt even with the sacrifice of life is better than a passive existence that accepts a slavery, dulled by physical pleasures and anaesthetised by superstition, as we see in the Blackamoor worshipping his coconut as a god and then slaying it. Freud, Marx, Fraser, the Gospel; you can take your choice or merely enjoy the movement and colour. Quite rightly none of its collaborators would make an explanation or comment. They allowed the work to speak for itself; it has done so for over half a century.

Petrouchka, the greatest of all dance dramas, bears witness to the immense dramatic possibilities in ballet, yet it is complete on the stage without the need of a single programme note.

The origin of the work shows the atmosphere in which ballet can be created, but only the atmosphere, since it is far from clear who actually created it. It was in fact the perfect collaboration of Fokine, Stravinsky and Benois chez Diaghilev where the atmosphere was as close to that in a Renaissance court, with its resident artists, as could exist in modern times.

Stravinsky had composed music round the theme of the legendary Russian figure *Petrouchka*. He had conceived the idea while waiting to begin *Le Sacre du Printemps,* which though produced later was already planned. He saw 'a puppet suddenly let loose who, by his cascades of fiendish arpeggios, exasperates the orchestra, who in its turn answers him by some threatening fanfares. A terrible scuffle ensues, which reaches its crisis by the painful and complete collapse of the poor puppet.'

It is certain that the inspiration began with this idea of Stravinsky's and the music that expressed it. Diaghilev acclaimed it a work of genius, hastily summoned Benois, with whom he had had a serious quarrel. Benois had always been interested in puppets and puppet theatres, carving his puppet heads out of potatoes. He soon forgot his grievance and became enthusiastic. He conceived the figure of Petrouchka, not as the legendary sly and brutal Punch, but as the pathetic victim of circumstances. He set the scene at the Carnaval in Admiralty Square. Benois and Stravinsky wrote to one another at great length, exchanging ideas, and then met in St Petersburg for a series of sessions together with Stravinsky at the piano; he was the only person who could play the score. Stravinsky added some of the fairground characters, introducing many popular melodies into his score. After Stravinsky's departure, Benois set to work on his designs, soaking himself in the atmosphere of that most inspiring of cities. Then the choreographer came on the scene.

Fokine claims to have introduced additions and modifications and to have been moved to create by direct contact with the music rather than through the intervention of Benois, the librettist and designer. From my knowledge of him he was certainly responsible for the characterisation of the figures in the crowd. The personalities of Karsavina, in my experience the only perfect doll, and of Nijinsky played their part, though Fokine states that they only followed his instructions. No matter, this is the perfect setting for the creation of ballet, and one almost impossible to achieve at the present day. I have not mentioned Diaghilev as a member of this team. His role was positive but invisible, and largely unacknowledged by the others. It was he who discovered Stravinsky and called in Benois and Fokine, giving them the necessary time for rehearsal, trial and error. He had the knowledge, prestige, and authority and, without doubt, from my observation at a later date, must have been responsible for some of the ideas. Certainly in the many post-Diaghilev revivals Benois' decorative afterthoughts have been far less successful. Diaghilev's only acknowledged role was to light the ballet. He was a master of theatrical lighting.

The ballet librettist, whether he be a poet, a designer, composer or choreographer, requires the guidance of a strong art director and the give and take of argument in sorting out his ideas. As we have seen, this great work was altered many times before its completion, not only in its setting but in the depiction of the central character.

The librettist cannot sit down and compose in his study. He needs the entourage of a ballet company, the society of composers, designers and choreographers. The greatest ballet dramaturgists have from Molière to Cocteau all been men of the theatre. The last of the great creators, Boris Kochno, was Diaghilev's lieutenant. His works enhanced the prestige of Massine and Balanchine, they made the young Roland Petit who followed in his footsteps. It is in France that writing ballets has flourished, because in France the arts that make up ballet march together. There is a romantic movement, a realistic movement, an impressionist movement, a fauve movement, a dadaist movement and so on in music, painting and literature. Beaudelaire and Hugo are draughtsmen, and few poets have not written a monograph on painting or music. In England the arts are kept in watertight compartments. With the exception of the Sitwells, who in France would have been constantly used in ballet, there are few writers really equipped to collaborate. Our ballet should gather round it the poets who could embellish it and express themselves in the medium of the dance.

In the Soviet Union there has been much discussion about ballet dramaturgy, and one poet, Pushkin, has become a posthumous inspiration for several generations. Could we have used Byron here? Today, however, in Russia the librettist assiduously cobbles the material for full evening ballets, always competent, carefully obeying the rules, but all too rarely inspired. He is a professional and that is already something.

The most dangerous assumption is that a 'hunch' will work and that it will all come out all right on the night. It never does. The ballet unless it is without theme or story, is made or marred by its argument. I quote two examples of what undoubtedly seemed good ideas when first mooted.

Sherlock Holmes is a household word, a character instantly recognised by all. Splendid, let us have a Sherlock Holmes ballet. But where does one go from there? There is an admirable Sherlock Holmes public house with a period setting and a museum of the great detective's triumphs, including the pickled body of the speckled band, the slipper tobacco pouch, the fiddle and the hypodermic syringe. Could a ballet give us more than that? Obviously not. Sherlock Holmes is an ingenious plot incapable of explanation without words. Sherlock Holmes is dialogue in which Watson, the greatest of all foils, is put in his place. Sherlock Holmes is the rumble of hansom cabs on cobbles and the sudden ringing of the Baker Street door bell. By no conceivable means could any of this be translated into ballet.

At first sight *Alice in Wonderland* seemed to hold far greater promise. It is a dream fantasy, and dreams are the very lifeblood of ballet. But once again a knowledge of the work should have shown how intractable was the material. Everything here depends on the clear use of language, on the particular mirror-world logic and the endless discussions. How can one render such unforgettable phrases as 'Sure then I'm here! Digging for apples, your honour' – 'What do you mean by that?' said the Caterpillar sternly, 'explain yourself'. 'I can't explain *myself*, I'm afraid, sir, because I'm not myself you see' – 'You can draw water out of a water well, so I should think you could draw treacle out of a treacle-well, eh, stupid?'

All of which is even more puzzling to the unfortunate dancer and the audience than, 'Elementary, my dear Watson'. Leave all of it out and what remains is a *tableau vivant* based on Tenniel's drawings, but without his fantasy. Yet this, too, seemed a good idea to someone. And, alas, such examples of 'hunch ballets' could be multiplied indefinitely.

Ballet and Opera are often compared. Apart from the fact that they share an opera house stage, there is no analogy. Opera uses words in addition to music and drama. It is in a sense the most *realistic* branch of theatre. In a duet we can have the simultaneous thoughts of the characters revealed and a complexity of emotions and situations such as in *The Ring,* where past, present and future coexist as in no other art form.

I have on many occasions, for the writing of pro-gramme notes, seen a completed ballet, and have attempted to set down what I saw. It is a difficult test. At times the impressions were vivid enough, the imagination had been stirred, but it was quite impossible to reduce it all to words. I can think of one particular ballet, *Cotillon,* a masterpiece by Kochno and Balan-chine. The setting was a straight-forward masquerade. Beneath the surface all sorts of things occurred; there was an atmosphere of disquiet, even of fear, but what actually happened, I never learned. Every time I saw it, it made a different impression. It had a logic in action but not in words. It was clear in action, there was an atmosphere but no narrative.

Programme notes, if necessary, are best kept to a bare minimum; characteristically Fokine said that he only included them for the sake of the critics.

Reason why classics are still performed today?

9 : *The Role of the Composer*

THERE are three relationships possible between music and movement in ballet.

The first is unsubtle and direct; when the music acts as a guide in tempo. Whether such music is made by the dancers themselves, drumming, clapping and stamping, or coloured by an orchestra playing the music of some hack, it is very much the same thing. Perhaps I was not completely accurate in writing unsubtle, since the drum could and, in the Indian dance does, set rhythms of such complexity that they are real mathematical problems. Where ballet is concerned my statement can stand.

The second relationship is the reverse of this, where the choreographer first composes his ballet and the composer then writes the music around it. I have only seen this done once, but with striking effect: in Serge Lifar's ballet *Icare*, where Honegger composed the

14. 'Ballet Faces' Senior pupils at the Leningrad Ballet School (*Mike Davis*)

15. Ekaterina Maximova in *Petrouchka* (L. Dubilt)

music to fit the finished work. It is not something that can be often repeated without disaster.

The third and natural relationship is where the music provides the atmosphere, follows the action, and sets the whole scene.

As one might imagine from what has transpired it was Noverre who anticipated all choreographers in his relationship with the composer. He writes, 'I composed, if I may express myself thus, the dialogue of my ballet. ... It was in this way that I dictated to Gluck the characteristic air of the ballet of the savages in *Iphigénie en Tauride;* the steps, the gestures, the attitudes, the expression of the various characters that I drew for him gave this celebrated composer the style of the composition of this beautiful music.'

Ballet music is a great deal more than incidental music. In a wordless play it is either a part of the libretto or, as in *Les Sylphides, Sérénade* and *Symphonic Variations,* the libretto itself. That is the reason why the term *abstract* ballet, often used for such storyless works, is completely inaccurate. What I will call *libretto-music* can either be already composed or specially commissioned.

The use of already composed music is frequent, usually for reasons of time and economy. It is only desirable when the choreographer is directly inspired by the music, as were Fokine, Balanchine and Ashton in the cases I have mentioned, and never, or scarcely ever, when it comes in as an afterthought to fit a theme or story that has already been fully conceived.

In the first case the choreographer is only doing what so many of us do at a concert, imagining a programme

G

for the music, with the difference that he does this with a trained mind.

In using ready-made music there are certain definite rules. The music itself, if it is of any quality, must never be cut and altered or played at the wrong tempo, Balanchine, who is inspired by much already existing music, has always insisted that the conductor must have the last word. In commissioned music, on the other hand, there is some latitude, especially in the classics where each classical ballerina has her own individual tempo. It is dangerous to select music that is so well known that people have already created their own images.

In the case of *Les Sylphides* there is certainly a distortion of essentially pianistic music through orchestration, and the purist could make out a case against it and did so, in the early days. However, the musical purist cannot be allowed to have the last word in what is a theatrical art. There can be no doubt that the music suffers some loss, but this is offset by the gain of a great work that in no sense does violence to the spirit of the music. The orchestration of piano music is in any case current practice and it might be, and indeed it is, argued that it is wrong to play Bach on the piano.

The great argument centres round the use of certain music that has been called *absolute,* music that is so complete in itself that movement can add nothing new and so becomes a distraction. This argument rose to great heights in the early 1930s with Massine's symphonic ballets. To take the discussion at the two extremes, the dancers claimed that any music that inspired them to movement was fair game, the musicians retorted that this was vandalism. It is not as simple as that. In two of the cases there could be no real argument. Massine's *Les Présages* was set to Tchaikovsky's Fourth Symphony. Tchaikovsky was a ballet composer, and this very music had originally been criticised as being too balletic. The second ballet was the Berlioz *Symphonie Fantastique,* but here the composer had conceived his own programme which Massine closely followed. The only debatable case was *Choreartium,* to Brahms' Fourth Symphony. Here Massine gave many striking moments of correspondence between music and movement, but the fit was not complete. Later in Beethoven's *Seventh Symphony* he failed. Perhaps for the reason that, as Wagner had already called one of its movements 'the apotheosis of the dance', to add dancing was mere decoration, which is not the function of ballet.

The main point in the whole argument is one of theatrical timing. In the symphony the composer develops his theme at great length and resolves it at leisure. The dancer cannot hold the audience at such length, the difference in time between what the eye sees and the ear hears is too great and there are inevitably long moments of repetition, much padding and boredom. This timing of ballets is incredibly deceptive. In all the great classical works, effective variations last from thirty seconds to three minutes, and the set piece *adagio* itself rarely lasts more than five minutes. In symphonic music, with few exceptions, the Bizet symphony is a striking one, the musical climax and the dance climax cannot be made to coincide.

Music to be suitable for ballet must have an urgent and direct quality. Rimsky Korsakov's *Schéhérazade* is a striking example. There was a definite programme in the composer's mind from which Fokine departed. No matter, the shipwreck of Sinbad became the massacre of the slaves, the incentive to violent action was there. Its sequel, Balakirev's *Thamar*, certainly better music, was not so successful a ballet. The music was less direct, less indicative of action in the present.

In specially composed music the same problems exist but to a lesser extent, especially when there is such complete collaboration as existed between Tchaikovsky and Fokine, Stravinsky, Fokine and Balanchine, and more recently, Prokofiev and Lavrovsky. The composers are familiar with the medium and with the choreographer's intentions. Petipa stood by the piano as Tchaikovsky played, dancing and miming and indicating bar by bar the music that he required. The composer can allow for lifts, always a difficulty in using ready-made music, and for the time the dancer requires to perform certain steps. The commissioned composer must remember that he is a member of a team and is not writing for the concert hall. That most successful composer of many ballets, Arthur Bliss, in his first work *Checkmate* wrote at too great a length. Some lengthy cuts doubled the dramatic intensity of the ballet without damaging the music. The composer was there to make the cuts. The fault of many contemporary ballets is their length, very few would not benefit through being condensed. French composers – Poulenc, Auric, Milhaud, Sauguet – have been particularly successful in writing for ballet. Once again it is the example set by Diaghilev. This question of length does not apply to the actual duration of the ballet – *Swan Lake* is a very long work

– but to the timing of the dances that make up the ballet.

The greatest contemporary composer of music for the dramatic ballet has been Prokofiev. No choreographer has failed in the numerous versions that have been made of *Romeo and Juliet,* so urgent, direct and inevitable is the progress of his score and so attractive and evocative his themes. He is a master storyteller in music. Curiously enough like Tchaikovsky, whose heir he was, *Romeo and Juliet* was considered too difficult for many years just as *Swan Lake* had been.

The best music is not necessarily the best ballet music, as we have already seen in the case of *Giselle*. Ravel's *Daphnis and Chloe* is one of the finest scores ever commissioned for ballet, but it is by no means the best ballet music, and is far more evocative in the concert hall.

We must, however, dismiss music churned out by professional hacks who may know all the tricks of timing but who have absolutely nothing to say. 'They insert a waltz every twenty minutes for safety,' as Prince Wolkonsky once said, and that is all. It is because of the vacuity of their music that the great majority of Petipa's ballets have disappeared. *Corsaire,* a ballet with an exciting and colourful story, is scarcely bearable for a whole evening. Adam's music fell far below the level of his *Giselle*. It is the same with the numberless ballets by Minkus and Pugni.

At times choreographers have revolted against music, claiming that their art must be free and independent. We have had ballets with no music at all. These occasional gimmicks have had but a passing interest. They have little hold on the audience, a cough, a giggle or an upset matinée tray and the mood has vanished

101

beyond recapture. For better or for worse the dance and music are lifelong partners.

There is one other consideration of an urgent and practical nature. Ideally ballet requires a full symphony orchestra. This is only practical when a company is attached to an opera house. The cost in rehearsal and performance is astronomic. Companies without a large subsidy and a permanent home must make do with a small scratch orchestra. The result is usually lamentable, and few touring companies are able to give performances that in any way approach those in a capital city. Apart from the sound produced, the dancers cannot possibly give inspired performances. A solution would be the use of two pianos. This would be bearable, but is very much a second best. Ballet needs a volume of sound and the colour of orchestration if it is really to succeed in the theatre. In any case the audience always insists on an orchestra, however inadequate it may be. Taped music, the best solution, is but rarely allowed by the trade's unions for reasons that can be appreciated. The problem cannot be solved.

10 : *The Role of the Painter*

IN ballet the role of the painter is different from that in any other branch of the theatre. The painter does not embellish a work that is complete in itself, he does not make the frame for a picture that is already painted, he is an equal partner in the making of the ballet.

Many plays are over-decorated so that little or nothing remains for the imagination. Many plays need no scenery in order to come to life. In Shakespeare the poetry sets the scene. *Hamlet* in modern dress is valid, or would be, if it did not in a sense underline the dress by drawing our attention to it so aggressively. But imagine *Giselle* on a bare stage with its whitewashed brick back wall, complete with NO SMOKING sign, its *wilis* in woollies and its hero in a sports jacket and corduroys. It would be laughable and unintelligible.

In 1933 Colonel de Basil presented a very successful ballet, already mentioned in another connection, *Les*

Présages. This had a very distinguished set by Joàn Miro, but the public eye was not yet focused to such abstraction and expressed a wish to see the ballet unfettered by décors in order better to appreciate the choreography. De Basil gave one such performance, not under the harsh conditions I have mentioned but with his dancers in neat practice costume against a well-lit cyclorama. Far from revealing the choreography, it practically extinguished it. Fate and Frivolity were dancers in the classroom performing difficult steps, in spite of the rhythmic strength of Léon Woizikovski and the lightness of Tatiana Riabouchinska. This was practice and not performance. And strangely enough the orchestra sounded too loud and out of place. With one element missing the whole fabric fell to pieces. The first to cry out against the décors now demanded their return. There could have been no greater demonstration of what is ballet.

The scenic designer's great problem, like the composer's, is to remember that he is not alone in the production. The backcloth is not a picture complete in itself. When it holds the attention too closely it detracts from the choreography. Chagall has not been a successful artist for ballet, neither has Salvador Dali for that very reason, though under the critical tutelage of Diaghilev they would surely have produced something noteworthy. For the same reason it was wrong to use a painting by Corot as a setting for *Les Sylphides*. It seemed a good idea at first until one remembered that Corot had painted Sylphs before Fokine was born. It was Diaghilev who returned to the practice of the Renaissance, and who commissioned décors from easel painters: Benois, Bakst, Korovin, Gontcharova, Larionov, Picasso, Matisse, Derain, Rouault, Tchelitchev and others. Previously, as in the case of the music, décors were commissioned from hack artists who produced more or less naturalistic sets that had become so completely standardised that members of the back row of the *corps de ballet* became known as 'the girls near the fountain', so inevitable was the garden scene with its fountain pumping real water. There is a precedent for this; was it not that inspired 'ham' Vincent Crummles who suggested to Nicholas Nickleby that he write a play round a property pump? He would have been at home in the ballet of his day. Diaghilev's easel artists became real theatrical craftsmen. Look at any of their costume sketches and you will see scraps of material pinned to the paper. They realise the effect of texture and the different values it will give to light, and the capacity of various materials for taking graceful shapes in movement. Very occasionally a painter merely indicates the type of thing he requires, in which case he needs a practised costumier to translate his designs.

The word *translate* is all important in another sense. A ballet often has a period or a place setting. *The Three Cornered Hat*, for instance, is situated in Spain. In Petipa's day there was a compromise style known as St Petersburg Spanish, pseudo-Spanish dancing in pseudo-Spanish costumes, as seen in the Spanish divertissement in *Swan Lake*.

One of Fokine's main reforms was to postulate a complete consistency of style. This did not mean the adoption of actual folk costumes, *naturalism,* but an interpretation. An actual horse would be *unreal* in the fantasy setting of *Le Coq d'or,* while a plywood steed is what the scene demands. It is the same with costume. The peasant costume is meant to be seen at close quarters out of doors in the sunlight. It needs translation for the stage. When a Spanish company produced *The Three Cornered Hat* in correct costume with folk music, the result was not only bad theatre but seemed curiously un-Spanish. In Massine's great ballet the dancing was stylised, the folk melodies were orchestrated by de Falla and the costumes stylised by Picasso. *Nothing was natural but everything was real.* The Spanish public acclaimed it. In period pieces this is equally valid, since the style of the dances of any period is dictated by the costume. There must be modifications for ballet dancing, but the essential style must be preserved, as it has been in Rex Whistler's brilliant translation of Hogarth in *The Rake's Progress.*

The scenic designer is not concerned with a single picture but with a gallery of paintings. Once again the French excel. All too often in England the effect is bitty; there are a few beautiful but over-decorated costumes that do not fit into the composition as a whole. The male dancer usually falls a victim. Sophie Fedorovitch was an outstanding exception, and her collaboration with Frederick Ashton saw many very distinguished works, designs that were simple in the grand manner and truly *musical,* notably *Symphonic Variations.* Just as the choreographer has to interpret music, so must his designer. The modern abstract painter has a considerable role to play in the non-story ballet where a mood is to be exploited, and no concrete place or time is demanded. The Russians, Larionov and Goncharova, under the inevitable aegis of Diaghilev, were pioneers in introducing modern art to the ballet. The contemporary Russians are inclined to stop at the naturalistic pre-Diaghilev grand spectacle, fountains and all, though recent ballets such as *Lieutenant Kije* have shown a change of direction.

It is often said that opera today is ahead of ballet in its settings. This may be true, when one thinks of a Zefirelli or a Visconti, but once again the two cannot be compared. The ballet designer can never forget the large space that dancing demands, the flat surface and the innumerable entrances and exits. He cannot play around with staircases and platforms to anything like the same extent. His basic plan remains very much a fixture. It is a hard discipline but, unlike choreography, one that could be taught in the colleges.

In ballet everything that is not necessary must be discarded. At one period there was a mania for ladders and scaffolding, introduced for their own sakes as a shock reaction against romanticism, a brutal assertion of the machine age. This is still seen occasionally. It dates even more than the prettiness of a misguided romanticism. The ballet that features a backstage setting, deliberately shattering illusion, has also had its day, though it was at one time an exciting novelty. The French word *décors,* suggesting decoration, misleads one as to the vital role of the painter in ballet.

11: *Ballet : The Whole*

We have now been through my definition in some detail, taken the parts to pieces and reassembled them. The result is an egg that, in spite of the Curate's dictum cannot be bad in parts.

We now face the question: Can this branch of theatre develop and continue to interest a modern audience? The great scenic painter, Natalia Goncharova gave one reply, that ballet was successful because it was the last stronghold of theatrical illusion. If by this she meant that ballet is pure escapism, one is forced to ask further questions, is it an art or merely an entertainment? Can it enrich life? Has it something that it alone can express?

Much nonsense is written about that pejorative word *escapism*. Reading a good book is escapism. Montaigne wrote that there was no sorrow that reading could not dull. Drugs, drink, golf, watching TV and the cinema, reading whodunits and crossword puzzles, are all escapism. Thank goodness for some means of escape.

We are concerned here with the level at which the escape is made?

When it leaves something behind it – other than a hangover or ashes and a fag end – when it is life-enhancing, enabling one the better to deal with the problems that come crowding in, when it purges the emotions but does not dull them, then, and then only, it can be taken seriously as an art. And then the escape is into reality. We have seen this taking place in *Petrouchka* and in many ballets, especially the classics, once the dancer has kissed them into life.

There is no reason to think that ballet will ever cease to attract an audience, even to increase its audience, so long as it remains true to the conventions I have outlined.

However, I do not believe that ballet will undergo many changes of form, though it will continue to reflect the atmosphere of its day and country. The classics will be lost if they are presented as museum pieces. They are rich enough to evolve with each period as they have shown in the transition from Tsarist to Soviet Russia. Great new ballets will of necessity be few and far between in an essentially ephemeral art; thirty years is a very long life-span for any ballet. Then there comes a change of fashion and it requires a long rest before the work can be reassessed for its positive values. The successful revival in 1964 of Nijinska's *Les Biches* was a case in point. In 1924 it spoke about its own days. Immediate revivals made it seem outmoded, but forty years later its setting can be accepted as belonging to history and its truth remains. An older ballet, *Schéhérazade,* magnificent in its choreographic pattern, fails because once the period exoticism ceases to exercise its magic, we are left with a melodrama. Noverre and Fokine set the formula for all time. The technique of ballet may develop, but only very little. There are limits to what the human body can do, and even in athletics, where the aim is always to beat records, it is now a matter of a fraction of a second at a time. In the past thirty years we have seen certain technical feats become commonplace and have been thrilled by the lifts of Soviet dancers. The ballerina of yesterday could not perform many steps required of the corps de ballet dancer of today. Paganini or Liszt could not perform much that is a commonplace to the musical student of today. This is a matter of quantity and not quality, and even so the quantity is comparatively small. The twist and other fashionable dances bring nothing that the African has not already explored. The Hindu classical dance has for the past two thousand years expressed emotions and conquered rhythms far beyond anything attained by the modern dancer. I have yet to see anything modern in the modern dance, admirable though some of it is.

This is neither to adopt a defeatist attitude, nor to write ballet down as something trivial. If the form of ballet itself and the technique of the dance remain static, there will always be ample material for the choreographer to draw upon and for the great dancer to illumine. Camargo, Sallé, Guimard, Taglioni, Elssler, Pavlova, Karsavina, Spessivtseva, Ulanova, Fonteyn, Chauviré, Vestris, Perrot, Nijinsky came out of and enriched the tradition. Noverre, Fokine, Balanchine, de Valois, Ashton made ballet a full and expressive art.

At this very moment their successors are clutching the *barre* with hot hands, taking part in the ritual exercises that are the foundation of their art. In some few there will be that spirit of revolt and adventure that beckons to them to create movement of their own.

Part III

12 : *Ballet Today :*
Some Problems

BALLET is run on a repertory system, the bill changing nightly, classics and modern works intermingled. The large company at a state opera house consists of a hundred or more dancers, principals, soloists and corps de ballet. All ballets undergo continual changes of cast which adds to the interest of a necessarily restricted repertoire. There are no stars imposed upon the audience by a vast publicity machine with its subsidised fan clubs and certainly no manufactured stars in the pop group manner. There can be no amateur dancers. Certain dancers are born stars and develop through hard work and skilled care; Ulanova, Plisetskaia and Vassiliev in Russia, Fonteyn in England, and Chauviré in France. Unlike opera singers, who rarely graduate from the chorus, ballet dancers usually proceed the hard way, through the ranks. They must first attract the attention of a choreographer, and then of the great public. And recognition must come quickly, the dancer is old at thirty-five unless he has already become a star, in which case he can continue as long as the public is ready to applaud. English and Russian audiences are faithful to their favourites, and, grateful for past enjoyments, tend to overlook the ravages of age. 'The tragedy of ballet,' said Ulanova, 'is that when the mind knows what to do, the body can no longer respond'. This is a limiting factor. It is all too rare to see a really mature artist as one does in opera, the legitimate theatre or in the concert hall. English and Russian audiences are wise in recognising that their old favourites, when great enough, can produce a quality that compensates for the loss of youth. How rare this is.

The company can exist without the star, and at times the star who shines too brightly for too long can damage the company, holding back the development of other dancers and causing harm to the box-office when he does not appear.

The star cannot exist in isolation without the company. When Nijinsky and Karsavina, and then Massine and Lopokova left him, Diaghilev continued to flourish. Even Pavlova, the greatest star of them all, surrounded herself with an expensive company, though doubtless she could have attracted an audience on her own. There are free-lance dancers who may appear from time to time as guest artists. They usually do so at a serious disadvantage to themselves and to the whole, unless they are outstanding enough to give every dancer in the company a lift.

A company is not composed of dancers trained at random, however brilliant they may be. Diaghilev was no exception to this rule. His dancers at his greatest period were trained in the Russian Imperial schools, and even later when the revolution had cut him off from this source, though the classical dancing declined, his dancers came from two or three Russian émigré schools that taught the Russian method. Markova and Dolin, for instance, were trained by a former St Petersburg trained dancer and member of his company, Seraphima Astafieva. for all his modernism Diaghilev never questioned the classical technique. He queried everything but that. Cecchetti remained his favourite teacher and Cecchetti was nothing if not conservative. Behind every company there is the school. The dancers have developed together, are taught according to a definite *school,* and the company becomes an individual with easily recognisable characteristics. Leningrad, Moscow, Paris, Copenhagen, Milan, London, New York; all have their highly individual styles.

Ballet is an immensely expensive undertaking and, when on the grand scale, beyond the resources of the commercial theatre. Like the iceberg, most of the bulk is invisible. There is the school with its dual staff, educational and vocational. There are the company maîtres de ballet, rehearsal pianists, stage managers and stage director. There is the wardrobe department and, for ballet, costumes need very constant renewal; a scene-painting department, and a large office staff for the complex business of touring. There is a full symphony orchestra and its conductors, and finally, what one sees, the dancers themselves and the production in which they appear which costs approximately between £5,000 and £7,000 an act. All of this demands, and on the Continent receives, a very large subsidy. Here also a good start has been made, though the powers-that-be will subsidise the end product without recognising the need for years of costly training. The Royal Ballet School is the only major ballet school in the world that depends on fee-paying pupils, which certainly complicates its task. Without subsidy, seats might cost from £7 to £12 each. Government or municipal spending is from a hard-headed point of view a sound proposition, prestige apart. It attracts foreign visitors and keeps them longer in the metropolis. A well-known company can tour the world and prove itself a considerable dollar earner, a vital consideration in these days of 'export or die'. Its school can attract foreign students in quantity. From the prestige point of view one has only to think of the record of Russian ballet since Diaghilev first came to western Europe in 1909. It served as a travelling exhibition of Russian painting and music, it drew attention to the riches of Russian literature. There is scarcely any memoir of this period written by an intellectual where the words *Russian Ballet* are not to be found in the index. It was, as we have seen, a deliberate aim of Benois and Diaghilev to make the ballet a show-case of Russian artistic achievement. And at the present time, when the Soviet Union is so often the bogeyman of the West, especially in the United States, the Bolshoi ballet, the Kirov ballet, the Moiseyev dancers and others are welcome guests, bringing the most civilised and the right sort of propaganda.

All of which wants stressing, since one often hears the type of argument that follows, if argument it can be called, and here I quote verbatim from the views expressed by a certain northern alderman: 'If people want opera and ballet and such like, let them pay for it. If it is really popular, they will, as they do for football and pop groups. If it is only liked by a few highbrows, I say, let it go.'

Such reactionary attitudes where the arts are concerned are the product of our history and geography. In Elizabethan times the English were noted for their love of music and dancing. A lute hung in many a barber's shop for the entertainment of waiting customers. People really danced on the village green. Morris dancing was not confined to the Albert Hall, and there was no need to invent a peasant costume. Then, with the Puritan revolution, the theatre became suspect, and dancing most of all.

The coming of our Industrial Revolution did away with a peasantry that danced and sang for its own amusement. A new class arose, skilled at money-making and not attuned to the arts. These men of substance, the Veneerings of *Our Mutual Friend,* invested in vast Royal Academy paintings and mahogany furniture as shiny and massive as their Albert-chained paunches.

With the coming of the railways London, the Great Wen, grew closer to the rest of England and, in any case, unlike the Continent, England had had no separate courts to rival one another by the magnificence of their opera houses. The Londoner, in many cases less wealthy than the midland or northern industrialist, spent money more freely. London attracted the best singers and dancers from abroad, applauded them and entertained them lavishly. London was a Mecca for the visiting artist, generous, and as Gautier said 'not over-critical'.

116

The brief ballet seasons became social events; exotic and not indigenous. An English artist found it hard to make a break-through, and on the rare occasions that he did it was under the safe disguise of a foreign name; for the singer Italian and, after 1910, Russian for the dancer.

It is sometimes not fully recognised how many English dancers there were before de Valois' break-through, and Diaghilev did not advertise the fact. Like Madame Mantalini all felt that an English appellation would be of serious injury to the business: Sokolova from 1912, and in the 'twenties, Markova, Dolin, Savina and some seventy-five per cent of Pavlova's company when Boot became Butsova. This is all past history. Ninette de Valois, her own name hidden, changed all that in a remarkably short time, the war providing the same opportunity that the patriotic war of 1812 had given the Russians.

Today the English compete on equal terms. However, a hangover remains and it is serious.

The Royal Ballet flourishes in London. In the provinces it dances, as I have already said, to inferior music. And because its visits to any one town are few and far between, the taste of the audience is a restricted one. They want something that is familiar, something that means ballet to them, the *ballet blanc*. The new repertoire rarely draws big houses. They want stars whose names are familiar, and hesitate to make their own discoveries, surely one of the excitements of ballet. To make matters worse, there are few large-stage theatres, even the big cinema houses are closing or are bingo-infested. Those that remain are concerned for some three months of the year with something, to which

117

children take their parents, miscalled a pantomime.

Since the Festival of Britain, as a partial remedy, many centres hold Festivals, admirable institutions, generally heartily disliked by the myopic locals as interfering with their amenities. The Festival is an incomplete solution; good theatre and opera, and in our case, good ballet, should not be an exceptional event but a part of life. To concentrate 'culture' into ten days of the year, a sop to the conscience, only underlines that 'culture' is no everyday concern.

England and America are the only countries where 'highbrow' and 'egg-head' exist as terms of abuse, so much so that the 'highbrow' apologises for himself and has recently taken to parading a cult for something that seems to embrace the best of both worlds, *pop art*. Label men in this selfconscious way and the 'low brow' becomes an inarticulate, comic-reading, grown-up child and the 'high brow' an emasculated freak in search of a gimmick, Ballet is a victim of such attitudes and prejudices.

An opera house cannot afford experiment. Every act of a new work costs at least £5,000 to mount, and is designed to take its place in the permanent repertoire. The big company must inevitably play for safety. There are small companies doing admirable work, but theirs is a hard life, and they lack stability. Ballet in England today requires three major companies, based in London, the midlands and the north, that is in addition to smaller experimental groups; companies that could develop dancers and choreographers, exchange visits and repertoires.

There are more dancing schools in England per head

of population than in any other country. There are a number of supervisory and examining bodies, headed by the Royal Academy of Dancing. There is a great source of supply in the Dominions. Many of these schools are, of course, grossly incompetent, but the good ones are very good and the standard is constantly rising. The majority of the pupils take a lesson a week, because it is the done thing, and have no professional ambition. They are valuable, however, as a future audience. The talent for three major companies exists, and today more dancers are produced than can find work. Some few are absorbed in musicals that now require fully trained ballet dancers, a few find casual work on television, some – alas, too many – teach an art that they have never had an opportunity of practising themselves.

One of the greatest problems today, outside Russia, is the short supply of male dancers, and without them ballet cannot flourish as a serious art. Gautier banished the male dancer as looking too much like a butcher boy, and the West has not yet fully reinstated him for the opposite reason, as looking insufficiently masculine. There are, of course, effeminate male dancers, and these are misfits, who do not fulfil their task, physically or dramatically.* It is not effeminate to dance, in primitive societies it is man who is the dancer.

There is also some confusion between romanticism and femininity. D'Artagnan wore lace, velvet and

---

* I believe that the prejudice against male dancers as being effeminate grew at the time our ballet was developing, during the war. Because of the call-up we had to rely on youths who were not effeminate but who were immature. The minute they gained maturity they joined the forces. Their war record was outstanding.

shoulder-length curls; no one would have called him effeminate and lived. It must be admitted though, that as far as England is concerned, costume designers have often been unkind to the male, and have themselves tended to confuse the romantic and the effeminate. The male dancer is of necessity a considerable athlete always in training, and recently the athlete has had recourse to the dancer, in learning various exercises that have been evolved from ballet technique. The prejudice is dying, but only very slowly in a society where there is no dancing peasantry and the folk dance requires a learned society for its preservation and encouragement. Ballet dancers are bored by a folk dance that is monotonous and artifically sustained, and the folk dance enthusiasts are less than enthusiastic about ballet, which they in their turn find artificial. That modern folk dance, the Twist, so loved by ballet dancers and the majority of young people, may yet help the recruitment of male dancers.

A final handicap, this time an economic one, is that outside Russia insufficient character dancers are used, and since dancers retire too early, ballets that require characters of weight lack the mature element that one saw in Lavrovsky's *Romeo and Juliet*. Our ballet world is one of extreme youth; mothers, nurses, tutors, kings and queens are scarcely out of their teens. These older artists are indispensable for a true dramatic balance. Who will ever forget the authority that Serge Grigoriev gave to the Shah in *Schéhérazade*, or to those burly Russian merchants he so often acted.

13 : *The Ballet :*
Screened or Boxed

Television

I HAVE stressed the fact that outside the capital city it is difficult to see much good ballet. As in the case of the dramatic theatre, television and the cinema have a role to play – a different and far less satisfactory role at this moment.

Television may be an enemy to all theatre. It keeps people at home, carpet-slippered and in the dry, in a comfortable armchair and with no need to dip into the pocket; that has already been done and is forgotten. The play is carefully pruned to last a short time so that there is no great concentration required. You can walk across the room to fill a pipe or brew a cup of tra. You can chatter throughout. You do not even have the strain of choosing your play. It has all been laid on. It is in fact magnificently cosy and it becomes a habit, a habit that keeps you away from the theatre. It kindles a false set of values, manufacturing 'celebrities' with conveyor-belt regularity. And I write as a TV addict, but a selective one, I believe.

That pessimistic view is not altogether true. The television play may develop a love for the theatre through serving as an introduction. There is no doubt that the broadcasting of good music helped to fill concert halls. Certainly in my experience the televising of ballet is excellent propaganda, both for ballet itself and for dancing as a career. Here, unlike the legitimate theatre, we have something not generally familiar and therefore a little suspect. People find that they like the small sample shown them, that this is not some mysterious esoteric cult and that it can therefore be safely patronised when it visits them, or when they are next in London. 'Saw it on the telly' is one of the most frequent replies to the question asked at an audition: 'What made you think of dancing?' Television sells detergents and chocolates, why not ballet?

This does not answer the question as to whether ballet on television is a good thing in itself. When live, it has the advantage that you are watching an actual performance with all the excitement that it may bring. A shoe flying off or the fall of a dancer are reassuring: 'This is the real thing and I am there, tonight.' When I took Fokine to see the first television performance of one of his ballets, *Carnaval*, He completely ignored the medium and made his usual notes on details of dance and costume. The television screen is a viewing window. In the case of some great public event it is a magnificent grandstand, enabling you to cover miles in a flash, and to have eyes at the back of your head. You are, however, watching the actual and not the contrived. The many cameras have solved the problem of space. When you talk of *seeing the boat race,* you really mean *seeing the boat race,* and not seeing the start, the middle or the finish.

With ballet it is entirely different. Ballet was designed for a stage, must be seen from the auditorium and not from the wings or backstage. Too many producers suffer from the Degas fixation. The dancers move rapidly, either jumping in the air or dancing across a very restricted space. It is easy to lose them altogether, or to cut out hands or feet. Even with a perfectly rehearsed show, where the camera never lost or truncated its dancer, it is quite impossible to concentrate on two principals leaping or circling the stage in different directions, or on the principals and the whole corps de ballet. This could only be done by a camera so far removed that the dancers become dots. Therefore someone has to decide for you what it is you are going to see – it is different in the boat race, where you are concerned with information – and that someone must also distort a very carefully planned composition to show it to you at all. In cutting out bits of the composition, he is also possibly interfering between the music and the flow of the movement. He can show you Giselle's folly, but not at the same time how it affected the others. He must switch from group to group and this is disturbing. Colour is an important part of ballet, on television it has yet to come. It is remarkable, therefore, with all these very real difficulties, how many good results have been obtained, especially by a television director trained in ballet, such as Margaret Dale. Her *Rake's Progress,* so well suited to the medium, was a landmark.

But however good the results, they are always a second best. There is, however, the possibility of something else, *television ballet* as distinct from *televised ballet*. Television to date has given us an enormous amount of dancing. It has become the last stronghold of a type of dancing that flourished when the writer was a schoolboy. It was then called 'musical comedy dancing', and consisted of kick right, kick left, link arms and grin. At its most efficient the girls, who themselves seemed factory-made, became a machine, but who in their senses wants girls to become a machine? The American musical, beginning with *Oklahoma,* killed this completely untheatrical nonsense, substituting classical ballet, leavened by modern dance techniques, and that became an integral part of the drama. One has only to think of the tremendous impact of the 'rumble' in *West Side Story.** Yet the old routines reappear on television screens with monotonous regularity, in programmes seriously misnamed variety. Television choreography is rare, but it has possibilities.

The Cinema

Ballet on the screen has its own problems.

The film has colour, a large screen and the possibility of taking in the whole. On the other hand it is contrived, and it loses the thrill of watching what may be the performance of performances. It is synthetic, made up of minutes of dance, taken over a long period and joined

* All this was hailed as a novelty, but, as we have seen, it was consciously developed by Molière.

124

together by an editor. The dancer does not adapt himself easily to constant interruptions. The same may be the case for the stage actor, but in dancing there is the added physical difficulty of stop and go. You may achieve mechanical perfection in this way, you may even introduce it by such devices as turntables, but mechanics are not enough. The only method that has overcome these difficulties is that devised by Dr Paul Czinner, which is to use a number of cameras to record an actual uninterrupted performance. He obtained a brilliant result with Ulanova's epoch-making interpretation of Giselle. The music was recorded at one performance and played back for the actual shooting, allowing for the natural applause and the stimulus it had on the dancers. Thus one great occasion has been handed down to posterity with all its genius and its imperfections. In spite of this film being shot at practically a moment's notice, the result was particularly satisfying. The selection of shots was never made disturbing through tricky camera changes, and the camera remained in the auditorium where the spectator belongs; only occasionally was he moved to a better seat. To do this requires a high degree of skill, a knowledge of ballet and music, as well as of the camera itself.

In the case of the same director's filming of Margot Fonteyn in *Ondine* some detail was revealed in the shadow dance, for instance, that made an even greater impression than in actuality. It is, however, a record that belongs to the archives, and still a second best to watching the actual performance. This is making use of the craft of cinematography and not of the art of the cinema. The Czinner films show his astonishing craft and

125

the difficulties he has so ingeniously concealed when one compares them to the Havelock Allen – Anthony Asquith *Evening at the Royal Ballet*. also filmed direct on the stage at Covent Garden.

There is another compromise method that the Soviet cinema has used on many occasions. That is to film an extended stage performance, using some cinematic tricks. The result is restless in the extreme, and one never knows where reality lies. Are we on the stage, or in the middle of a real lake? Is this the stage or the solid structure of Capulet's palace? And the dancers seem in as great a state of doubt as we are. Some of these Soviet films have beautiful dance sequences, notably in *Romeo and Juliet,* but they are sequences and not the ballet as we know it.

Cine-choreography has been tried on occasions with imagination, notably in musicals, and never better than in those unforgettable works by Fred Astaire, in particular the *Dancing in the Rain* sequence, also in ballets by Balanchine, such as *Slaughter on Tenth Avenue* or the skit on such exotics as *Schéhérazade,* and some sequences from Gene Kelly's ambitious *Invitation to the Dance*. These represent a perfect translation of ballet into a new medium, a fusion of two theatre arts. The movement of the dancers and of the cameras both flow from the music and are never antagonistic. Jerome Robbins' *On the Town* and his *West Side Story* were equally cinematic, the latter making an even stronger impact than in the original stage presentation. A great feat when one had seen the original.

A more serious approach had been given to the famous

126

ballet in *The Red Shoes*. Yet it was as false as the ballet story of which it formed a part. Dancers, muscles flexed through contact with the stage, floated unconvincingly in space. There were more 'gimmicks' than in the most dated romantic period ballet, and as little sense of reality. True, this was a dream, but not of the sort that anyone in the audience might have dreamed.

The only story with a ballet setting and with ballets introduced that has reached perfection was the French, *La Mort du Cygne*, with Yvette Chauviré, at the beginning of her great career, Mia Slavenska, and an unknown child, later to become famous, Janine Charrat. This was the truth. Unfortunately, it was bought up by Hollywood and butchered until only the name remained.

It is to be hoped that the much discussed film of Nijinsky's life never takes place. We have already suffered from *ersatz* Pavlovas. The whole idea is impossible from the start. Nijinsky was Nijinsky. It is true that Napoleon was Napoleon, etc., but there can be no comparison. The scope is so much greater, there are infinite possibilities for action. In this case it is not an actor assuming the role of a man of action, but one dancer pretending to be another, as if Montgomery played Wellington or Harold Wilson Gladstone. Nijinsky's raison d'etre was his dancing; take that away and you have nothing. If his role is taken by a mediocre dancer, it is ridiculous, if by a great dancer, it is something entirely different; and the great dancer will spend the rest of his life labelled as a facsimile, a second Nijinsky. The only motive there can be for making such a film is a commerical one, and while box-office is a consideration in every branch of the theatre, when it is the only one, it does not produce worth-while results. A still photograph of Nijinsky tells us more about him than a hundred movies.

The cinema could present the fusion of the arts that has been aimed at for so many centuries, and at its least pretentious it has come close to it. The early camera work that recorded the chases of the Keystone Cops, Chaplin in his unforgettable dance with the globe in *The Great Dictator,* indeed Chaplin in all his works, shuffling into the distance, his back more expressive than a hundred close-ups, pointed the direction. The field is still wide open.

16. Vladimir Vasiliev in *Narcissus* (*V. Bliokh*)
17. Ekaterina Maximova as Maria in *The Fountain of Bakhchisarai* (*APN*)

18. Dudinskaya leading the Kirov Ballet Company class (*Mike Davis*)

14 : *Dance Criticism*

DANCE Criticism, as opposed to the writing of professionals, is of comparatively recent date, though many great writers, Voltaire among them, have written revealingly of ballet. Certain names stand out, notably that of Théophile Gautier, who has left a vivid picture of the dancers of his day with such telling phrases as: 'Fanny Elssler's dancing bears a personal stamp which distinguishes her from all other dancers; it is not Taglioni's aerial and virginal grace; it is something much more *human* which appeals more acutely to the *senses*. Mlle Taglioni is a Christian dancer . . . Mlle Elssler is entirely a pagan dancer.' In his advice to the too-smiling Grahn 'a smile should hover about a dancer's lips like a bird about a rose'.

Gautier has no philosophy of ballet and is often inconsistent. He is a great critic because he is a poet who can translate ballet into words. His dancers still live in his writings. His is a champion of art for art's sake. 'Dancing after all has no other object but the revelation of beautiful forms in graceful attitudes and the development of line agreeable to the eye.' He is suspicious of emotion, form is everything. He is a voluptuary; 'the first condition required in a dancer is beauty; she has no excuse for not being beautiful and she can be blamed for her plainness as an actress can be blamed for bad pronunciation'. His criticism invariably starts with a physical description of the dancer. Yet, in spite of this, he attaches importance to the libretto and continually stresses its difficulties.

Poetic criticism, without the knowledge of Gautier, has been a feature of French writing from Gautier's time onwards, coming to a climax with the paeans of praise that greeted Diaghilev with Karsavina and Nijinsky. It reads magnificently, and, as I have found in practice, completely defies translation.

The old Russian critics were more down to earth. Volyinsky learnt the technique of ballet at an advanced age and was a pioneer of the new Soviet ballet, Valerian Svetlov became the champion of Fokine and his neo-romanticism. André Levinson, the best writer on ballet of this century, followed Gautier's 'art for art's sake' outlook and was a bitter opponent of Fokine, whom he accused of over-stressing the subject matter in ballet.

Soviet critics, many of them dancers or choreographers, have, as one would imagine, a very positive philosophy that underlines the need for realism, for something that is life-enhancing, and for the necessity of a positive hero. The dance is a comment on nature. To quote that outstanding critic, Yuri Slonimsky, ballet must be 'the re-creation by means of choreography of the inner substance of the drama, of its conflicts'.

Soviet criticism, influenced by Stanislavsky, follows the path of Noverre and Fokine rather than that of Gautier. The majority of English and American critics today – the present writer is an exception – would subscribe to Gautier's dictum that the object of the dance is to reveal beautiful forms in graceful attitudes and the development of line agreeable to the eye, though they are not doctrinaire and are prepared to take a work on its own merits.

Ballet critics have a useful function to perform at a period when ballet is almost entirely controlled by dancers and choreographers, and when often 'one cannot see the ballet for the feet'. They hold a watching brief for ballet as a whole. The function is a difficult one by its very nature, since it is impossible to quote or illustrate, and the writer is concerned with music, choreography, dancing, theme and décors. Under existing conditions criticism is made still more difficult since all these elements must be judged at first sight and set down on paper immediately after the performance, with barely half an hour in which to do so. The first burning impression made on a trained mind has its value, but needs checking at leisure and with far more space than is available in a daily newspaper. Russian critics have both the time and almost unlimited space. However, we have gone a long way from the days, some twenty-five years ago, when ballet was dealt with by a music critic under the rubric 'this week's music'. Gautier felt that it was really the province of the art critic, but as I have already written, in France the arts are much more closely inter-related.

Where the critic sometimes fails is in understanding the nature of repertory ballet, and the type of work that can or cannot be performed on an opera house stage. The repertoire must be varied; it is in practice essential to use the cast available to the best advantage, resting some and extending others. The critic must judge only what he sees and need take no notice of managerial excuses, but when he offers advice to the management, the advice must bear actual conditions in mind, and at times it does not.

15 : *Information Please*

The Literature of Ballet

THERE is a vast literature of ballet, especially since the
1930s. The present writer has perpetrated many books
on the subject. The classics of ballet are, however,
exceptionally rare and difficult to obtain. Here are some
to which I am particularly indebted for stimulus and
information. I exclude my own from these!

JEAN NOVERRE. *Lettres sur la Danse,* 1760.
Though his examples are necessarily dated, his writing
is vivid and his pen dipped in acid. His precepts are still
invaluable both for the choreographer of ballet and
the modern dance. When they have been neglected ballet
has suffered. The best edition, a collector's item, is the
one published in St Petersburg in four volumes, 1803.
There is a French edition, introduced by André
Levinson, and an English translation by Cyril Beaumont,
1930. Derek Lynham wrote a biography of Noverre,
published in 1950.

THÉOPHILE GAUTIER *The Romantic Ballet.*
This is an English translation of Gautier's criticism, assembled, introduced and translated by Cyril Beaumont, 1932. An admirably vivid work, dealing with the period that set its stamp on ballet and that is still with us today. Gautier's dancers come to life and no writing on ballet, or rather, on dancers, is more illuminating.

IVOR GUEST *The Romantic Ballet in England,* 1954 *Fanny Cerrito,* 1956 *Victorian Ballet Girl,* 1957 *Ballet of the Second Empire,* 1949. 2 Volumes.
Mr Guest is an enthusiast and a historian, and these works are the result of considerable research among the newspapers of the day. Apart from being excellent reading they are a mine of information about the 'golden age' that preceded ours.

DEIRDRE PRIDDIN *The Art of the Dance in French Literature* 1952.
A remarkable book dealing with dance aesthetics and practical criticism from Gautier to Cocteau, Valéry and Bergson. The result of research that has rescued much valuable writing from newspapers and magazines. A necessity for the serious student, the critic, choreographer and dancer.

PAUL VALÉRY *L'Âme et le Danse.*
A dialogue between Socrates and his friends that discusses in the most delicate, subtle and poetic manner the inner meaning of the dance. This work, by a great

poet, is more illuminating than any other writing, in spite of Éryximaque's reply to Socrates 'Que veux tu du plus clair sur la danse, que la danse elle-même?'

THE DIAGHILEV BALLET

TAMARA KARSAVINA *Theatre Street,* 1930.
No dancer has ever written a better book. It ranks with Stanislavsky's works on the theatre. It is intensely personal, written with enormous charm, yet it has a clear and detached viewpoint. It tells of what it meant to be a pupil of the Maryinsky School, St Petersburg, at one of the most creative periods in its history, and of becoming a member of Diaghilev's group when it revolutionised ballet. Karsavina created such roles as Thamar, the leading part in *Les Sylphides,* The Firebird, the Doll in *Petrouchka,* the Miller's wife in *The Three-Cornered Hat,* and the list is far from exhausted. She discusses the interpretation of these roles and the characters of the many remarkable artists in her entourage. And from a purely negative point of view, this is one of the rare theatrical memoirs that omits such trivia as 'what the King of Siam said to me' or 'the compliments paid to me by X. Y and Z'.

ALEXANDRE BENOIS *Memoirs,* Vol. II, 1964.
This deals with Benois' collaboration with Diaghilev and the early days of the ballet. Although written in old age, it brings back the excitement of those great creative days.

SERGE GRIGORIEV *The Diaghilev Ballet*, 1953.
This is indispensable as a day-to-day record of Diaghilev's activities by the man who was his stage director throughout his career, and who carries in his head all the ballets of the period, many of which he has revived for the Royal Ballet, among them *Les Sylphides, The Firebird* and *Petrouchka*.

PRINCE PETER LIEVEN *The Birth of Ballet Russes*, 1936.
An account of the early days of the Diaghilev Ballet, written largely from Benois' point of view.

ARNOLD HASKELL *Serge Diaghileff*, 1935.
This contains much material from Walter Nouvel, one of Diaghilev's closest collaborators.

FOKINE *Memoirs of a Ballet Master*. Edited Anatole Chujoy, 1961.
This consists of a memoir, together with many important articles and a detailed description of his works, their creation and interpretation. There is a still more complete Soviet edition, admirably illustrated and with a foreword by Yuri Slonimsky showing the present day Russian view of Fokine.

VICTOR DANDRÉ *Anna Pavlova in Life and Art*, 1932.
This account, written by Pavlova's husband, is in no sense critical. It contains much valuable information as well as many trivialities, but the illustrations are magnificent.

CONTEMPORARY BALLET

MARY CLARKE *The Sadler's Wells Ballet*, 1955.

SVEND KRAGH JACOBSON *The Royal Danish Ballet*, 1955.

YURI SLONIMSKY *The Bolshoi Theatre Ballet*, 1956.

ARNOLD HASKELL *The Russian Genius in Ballet*, 1963.

ANATOLE CHUJOY *The New York City Ballet*, 1953.

NINETTE DE VALOIS *Come Dance with Me*. 1957 Reminiscences and ideas by the founder of the Royal Ballet.

REFERENCE

CYRIL BEAUMONT *The Complete Book of Ballets*, 1937. *Supplement to the Complete Book of Ballets*, 1942.

ANATOLE CHUJOY *The Dance Encyclopaedia U.S.A.*, 1949

G.B.L. WILSON *Dictionary of Ballet*, 1957 (Penguin Books). A revised edition in hard covers, 1961.
Edited ARNOLD HASKELL *Ballet Annual*, from 1947 to 1964.

Iconography

CYRIL BEAUMONT and SACHEVERELL SIT-WELL *The Romantic Ballet in Lithographs of the Time,* 1938.

These lithographs are not of great artistic value, though they have an immense nostalgic charm. At their best, however, they are of considerable importance as showing us how their contemporaries viewed the outstanding ballerinas of this great period, and in this sense they have far greater reality than the photographs of today. The authors have assembled a magnificent and representative collection of works that could, only a few years ago, have been picked up for a few shillings and that are now expensive and scarce.

ARNOLD HASKELL *A Picture History of Ballet,* 1954.

ALBERT KAHN *Days with Ulanova,* 1963.

A remarkable record of the daily life of one dancer, photographed over a considerable period and revealing the personality of the artist and the setting and atmosphere of the Bolshoi Theatre and the Ballet School.

Edited PAUL MAGRIEL *Pavlova,* 1948. *Nijinsky,* 1948. *Isadora Duncan,* 1948.

MERLYN SEVERN *Ballet in Action,* 1938.
A record of the de Basil baby-ballerina period.

138

MICHAEL PETO and ALEXANDER BLAND
The Dancer's World With drawings by Joseph Herman,
1963. A record of the Royal Ballet in recent years.

PERIODICAL
The Dancing Times, monthly magazine, founded by the
late P. J. S. Richardson in 1910.

A Brief Chronology of Key Dates

1581 *Ballet Comique de la Reyne.* France, reign of
Henri III. Mentioned text page 31.

1588 Publication of Thoinot Arbeau's *Orchésographie,*
a detailed description of the social dances of the
day, prefaced by a dialogue on the value of
dancing. Arbeau's real name was Jehan Tabouret.
He was Canon of Langres; another link between
dancing and the Church.

1636 Opening of the theatre, Le Palais Cardinal.
Reign of Louis XIII.

1661 Foundation of l'Académie Royale de la Danse.
France, reign of Louis XIV. Mentioned in text
page 33.

1661 Molière's *Les Fâcheux,* his first comedy ballet,
shown at the memorable fête at Vaux where
'music, fountains, chandeliers and the stars vied
with one another for the King's pleasure'. This
fête saw the end of Fouquet's dazzling career. It
is described in fiction in Dumas' *Vicomte de
Bragelonne.*

1670 *Le Bourgeois Gentilhomme*. France, reign of Louis XIV. The use of ballet in Molières play as an integral part of the action and not as an interlude to rest the actors.

1672 Foundation of l'Académie Royale de Musique et de Danse. France, reign of Louis XIV, mentioned in text page 34. Date of the true birth of professional ballet.

1681 *Le Triomphe de l'amour*. France, reign of Louis XIV. Mentioned in text page 35. Marks the active participation of women in ballet.

1684 Publication of a small volume by the Jesuit Father Ménéstrier, a history of the dance and a first attempt at an aesthetic.

1701 Publication of Feuillet's *Chorégraphie, ou l'art d'écrire la danse par caractères, figures et signes demonstratifs*.

1708 Corneille's *Les Horaces* given at the château of La Duchesse de Maine, the first ballet to use a narrative drama. France, reign of Louis XIV.

1726 Debut of La Camargo. France, reign of Louis XV. Mentioned in text page 36.

1734 Marie Sallé dances *Pygmalion* in London. Reign of Louis XV. Mentioned in text page 36.

1735 Jean Baptiste Landé mounts a lavish spectacle in Russia for le corps des pages. St Petersburg. Reign of Empress Anne.

1748 Opening of the Royal Theatre, Copenhagen. The importance of Danish ballet began seven years later with the engagement of the Italian Vincenzo Galeotti. His ballet, *Les Caprices de Cupidon,* still holds an honoured place in the repertoire. It was Galeotti's successors, the Bournonvilles, who planted the characteristic Danish style, which is, in fact, the only survivor of the pure French style to be seen today.

1752 Landé founds the Imperial School at the Winter Palace, St Petersburg. Russia, reign of the Empress Anne. The birth of Russian Ballet.

1760 Publication of Noverre's *Lettres sur la danse.* See text page 38.

1773 Dancing classes started in the Moscow Orphanage, opened in 1764 to train children for the stage. Russia, reign of Catherine the Great.

1776 Catherine the Great appoints a director of the Imperial Theatres.

1783 The Moscow Orphanage school is moved to the Petrovsky Theatre, site of the present Bolshoi. Russia, reign of Catherine the Great.

1799 Ivan Valberg, the first Russian choreographer, produces a great novelty, the *New Werther,* a ballet in contemporary costume. Russia, reign of Paul I.

1801 Didelot comes to Russia and lays the foundation for the lavish spectacular Russian Ballet. Russia, reign of Paul I.

1812 Foundation under Carlo Blasis of the Milan Scuola di Balla.

1817 Adam Glouchkovsky, pupil of Didelot, is the first Russian choreographer to produce a ballet from contemporary literature. Pushkin was a great source of inspiration then as now. Russia, reign of Nicholas I.

1830 Publication of Blasis' *Code of Terpsichore,* the basis of modern ballet technique. Text page 40.

1832 Première of *La Sylphide* in Paris, beginning of the romantic ballet. France, reign of Louis-Philippe.

1841 Première of *Giselle.* France, reign of Louis-Philippe.

1869 Marius Petipa, who arrived in Russia in 1847, becomes ballet master of the Maryinsky Theatre, St Petersburg, a post he held until 1903. Russia, reign of Alexander II.

1870 Première in Paris of *Coppelia.* France, reign of Louis Napoleon.

1877 Première in Moscow of *Swan Lake.* Russia, reign of Alexander II.

1890 Première in St Petersburg of *The Sleeping Beauty.* Russia, reign of Alexander III.

1892 Première in St Petersburg of *Casse Noisette.* Russia, reign of Alexander III.

1895 Première in St Petersburg of the new production of *Swan Lake* by Petipa and Ivanov, the basis for all contemporary versions. Russia, reign of Alexander III.

1905 Isadora Duncan's first visit to Russia.

1907 Anna Pavlova's first tour, to Finland.

1909 Diaghilev's début in Paris, Théâtre du Châtelet, June 4th. The programme consisted of : *Cléopatre,* ballet by Fokine, décors Bakst and music by Arensky and others.
Le Pavillon d'Armide, book by Benois, choreography Fokine, décors by Benois, music by Tcherpnine.
Les Sylphides, theme and choreography by Fokine, music Chopin, décors Benois.

1911 Diaghilev's first visit to London.

1912 Nijinsky's choreographic début; *l'Après midi d'un faune.*

1917 Leonide Massine's choreographic début, *Les Contes Russes.*

1919 Agrippina Vaganova becomes director at the Leningrad School, forming the link between the old Russia and the new, a symbol of this is her statue facing that of Petipa in the large classroom in Rossi Street. The school today is known as the Vaganova Academy. Her teaching, set out in *Fundamentals of the Classic Dance,* is the basic method in the Soviet Union.

1921 *The Sleeping Beauty* at the Alhambra, London. See text page 58.

1923 Nijinska's first ballet for Diaghilev, *Les Noces.*

143

1925 Balanchine's first ballet for Diaghilev, a new version of *Le Chant du Rossignol,* the leading role created by an English child, Alicia Markova. Début of Marie Semenova, first great ballerina of the Soviet Union.

1928 Début of Galina Ulanova.

1929 Lifar's début as choreographer with a new version of *Le Renard.*
Diaghilev dies in Venice.

1930 Founding of the Camargo Society, the beginning of the English movement.
Founding of Ballet Rambert, first known as the Ballet Club, at the Mercury Theatre, Notting Hill Gate.

1931 Ninette de Valois founds the Vic-Wells ballet and school, afterwards the Sadler's Wells Ballet and now the Royal Ballet.
Serge Lifar becomes choreographer and premier danseur at the Paris Opéra.

1932 Colonel de Basil and René Blum start the Monte Carlo Ballet with the Diaghilev contingent of Grigoriev, Balanchine, Massine, Tchernicheva, Danilova, and the 'baby ballerinas' Baronova, Toumanova, Riabouchinska. The beginning of the Indian Summer of ballet-russe.

1933 Première of the de Basil Monte Carlo Ballet at the Alhambra, London.
Beginning of the final phase of ballet-russe. Programme, *Les Sylphides, Les Présages, Le Beau Danube.*
Frederick Ashton joins Sadler's Wells.

144

19. 'Break' Pupils of the Royal Ballet School, White Lodge, Richmond Park (*Mike Davis*)

20. 'In The Wings' Pupils from the Royal Danish Ballet School (*Mike Davis*)

1934 Lincoln Kirstein and George Balanchine start the American School of ballet, the beginning of an American national ballet.

1935 Alicia Markova leaves Sadler's Wells to found her own company.
The emergence of Margot Fonteyn.

1945 Les Ballets des Champs Elysées; artistic director Boris Kochno, introduces a new choreographer, Roland Petit.

1946 Sadler's Wells Ballet goes into residence at Covent Garden. A second company formed for Sadler's Wells.

1947 Sadler's Wells Ballet School in its own premises includes ballet and general education.

1948 Sadler's Wells Ballet's first tour of the U.S.A. Creation of Frederick Ashton's *Cinderella* (Prokofiev), the first full evening ballet in the new English repertoire.

1955 Sadler's Wells Junior School moves to White Lodge, Richmond Park.

1956 First visit of Bolshoi Ballet, with Ulanova, to Covent Garden.
Sadler's Wells Companies and School incorporated under Royal Charter.

1960 Visit of Kirov Ballet to Covent Garden.
The Royal Ballet visits Moscow and Leningrad.

1963 Second visit of the Bolshoi Ballet to London, with Maia Plisetskaya.

Ballets to be seen in the current repertoires

The basic repertoire of ballet is a restricted one, even compared with opera, where the big five, Mozart, Verdi, Wagner, Puccini and Strauss provide the bulk of repertoires all over the world. In drama, on the other hand, the field is so immense that one might go a lifetime without having an opportunity of seeing some of the greatest classics; Ibsen's *Brand*, for instance. They can always be read, but a ballet once out of the repertoire is dead. The student of ballet is never deprived of a chance of studying the classics, especially in Great Britain and the Soviet Union. The versions of these classics will vary not only from country to country but from company to company, but the basic classical form will remain intact, often even in the case of entirely fresh productions.

Pre-Diaghilev Ballets

Casse-Noisette (The Nutcracker). Music by Tchaikovsky, libretto and choreography by Lev Ivanov. First performed at the Maryinsky Theatre, St Petersburg, 1892. First performance of the complete work in western Europe at Sadler's Wells in 1934. Revived by the Festival Ballet in versions by Beriosov and Lichine and in 1954 for the New York City Ballet by Balanchine. The last act, *The Kingdom of Sweets,* is often given by itself, and the Sugar Plum variation is a favourite divertissement.

Coppelia. Music by Léo Delibes. Original choreography by A. St Léon; libretto by St Léon and Charles Nuitter

146

based on a story by E. T. Hoffmann. First performed in Paris in 1870, the last visit of Napoleon II and his Empress to the Opéra.

First performed in England in 1906 at the Empire with Adeline Genée as Swanilda.

It is sometimes given in two acts without the final wedding divertissement that adds nothing to the story. Swanilda is the supreme test of the soubrette. The role of the hero Franz was originally designed for a woman *en travesti*.

La Fille Mal Gardée (or *Vain Precautions*). Original music unknown. Choreography and story by Jean Dauberval. First performance in Bordeaux 1789. Remarkable as being a ballet about ordinary peasants at a time when gods and heroes monopolised the stage.

Was reproduced in 1828 with new music by Hérold and again in 1864 with music by Hertel.

It was first danced in England by Anna Pavlova in a shortened version.

It was produced by the Royal Ballet in 1960 with the Hérold music (arranged by J. Lanchberry) and with new choreography by Frederick Ashton. A survival from the production known in Russia was Lise's charming mimed scene from the last act which was shown to Ashton by Karsavina.

Giselle (or *Les Wilis*). Music by Adam. Libretto by Théophile Gautier and Saint Georges, suggested by a passage in Heine's *de l'Allemagne*. Choreography by Coralli and Perrot. First performed at the Opéra, Paris, 1841. The role of Giselle was created by Carlotta Grisi and Albrecht by Lucien Petipa. The first Russian

Giselle was Andreyanova (1842) and the first English Giselle, Markova (1934).

The role of Albrecht was greatly developed by Nijinsky. See text pages 46 and 51.

The Sleeping Beauty. Music by Tchaikovsky. Choreography by Petipa after Perrault's story. First performed at the Maryinsky Theatre, St Petersburg in 1890 with Carlotta Brianza as Princess Aurora, Pavel Gerdt as the Prince and Cecchetti as the Blue Bird.

Reproduced at the Alhambra, London by Diaghilev in 1921 under the title *The Sleeping Princess* with Brianza as the wicked fairy Carabosse. There was a new décor by Leon Bakst and some choreographic additions by Nijinska, notably the *Dance of the Three Ivans* in place of the *coda* of the pas de deux in the last act.

The ballet was revived by the Sadler's Wells company at that theatre in 1939 with décors by Nadia Benois. Margot Fonteyn as Aurora and Robert Helpmann as the Prince. It opened Covent Garden after the war in 1946 with the same leading dancers and new décors by Oliver Messel. It introduced Sadler's Wells to the U.S.A. (See text page 59.)

Swan Lake. Music by Tchaikovsky. First produced in Moscow in 1877 in a version that was a failure. The music was considered too symphonic and difficult for the dancers.

It became a success at the Maryinsky Theatre, St Petersburg, in 1895 with choreography by Petipa and Ivanov. Legnani created the roles of Odette and Odile and caused a sensation with her 32 fouettés.

148

It was revived in Moscow by Gorsky in 1901 and this version with additions by A. Messerer is the one seen there today A new and popular dramatic version by Bourmeister is given at the Stanislavsky Theatre, Moscow.

There have been a number of versions by the Royal Ballet in London since the first in 1934. The latest, produced at Covent Garden in 1964 by Robert Helpmann, has choreography by Frederick Ashton and some numbers by R. Nureyev. (See text page 73.)

La Sylphide. Music by Schneitzhöffer, choreography by Philip Taglioni, libretto by Nourrit. First performed Paris Opéra in 1832 with Taglioni as La Sylphide. Its success revolutionised ballet.

Bournonville did a version in 1836 with a new score by Lovenskjöld and this remains in the Copenhagen repertoire. It was revived for Marie Rambert's company in 1960.

Gsovsky mounted a version for the Ballets des Champs Elysées using the original music and with noteworthy décors by Christian Bérard. (See text page 45.)

Sylvia. Music by Delibes, choreography by Mérante, libretto by Barbier and Reinach. First performed at the Paris Opéra in 1876 with Rita Sangalli as Sylvia. It is a rare survivor from the ballet of this period.

It was the wish of Diaghilev and Benois to revive the ballet at the Maryinsky Theatre in 1900, but the plan failed.

It was revived in Paris in 1941 and was a personal triumph for Lycette Darsonval.

149

Frederick Ashton did a new production at Covent Garden in 1952 with Margot Fonteyn in the title role.

MODERN FULL-LENGTH BALLETS
(to be seen mainly in the Soviet Union)

Cinderella. Music by Prokofiev, choreography by Zakharov, Bolshoi Theatre, 1945 (title role created by Ulanova).

A version by Frederick Ashton, Royal Opera House, 1948.

(Perrault's tale has been the subject of many ballets.)

Romeo and Juliet. Music by Prokofiev, choreography by Lavrovsky. Kirov Theatre, 1940 (title role created by Ulanova). A version for the Royal Danish Ballet by Frederick Ashton 1955. A version for the Royal Ballet by Kenneth Macmillan 1965. Lifar has treated the subject in a one-act ballet to the Symphonic poem by Tchaikovsky.

Ondine. Music by Henze, choreography by Ashton, Covent Garden, 1958. (Ondine created by Margot Fonteyn.)

(This is inspired by Perrot's ballet of 1843 in which Cerrito made her name in the shadow dance, music by Pugni.)

Fountain of Bakhchisarai. Music by Asafiev, choreography by Zaharov. Kirov Theatre, 1934 (Ulanova created the role of Maria).

(Based on the poem by Pushkin.)

Laurentia. Music Krein, choreography, Chaboukiani. Kirov Theatre, 1939.

(Inspired by Lope de Vega's *Fuente Ovejuno.*)

The pas de six from this ballet revived by R. Nureyev for the Royal Ballet, 1965.

Path of Thunder. Music by Karaev, choreography by Sergeev. The libretto by Y. Slonimsky after the novel by Peter Abrahams. Kirov Theatre, 1957.

(This ballet deals with *apartheid*.)

Gayné. Music by Khatchaturian, choreography by Anisimova. Produced in 1942 by the Kirov company at Perm. (The setting is a collective farm.)

Spartacus. Music by Khatchaturian, choreography by Jacobson. Kirov Theatre, 1956, also given by the Bolshoi. (Story of the Slave Revolt in 73 B.C.)

Don Quixote. Music by Minkus, choreography by Petipa. Maryinsky Theatre, 1869. Revived in 1902 by Gorsky for Moscow. This version is the current one.

Given in England by the Rambert Ballet.

The famous *pas de deux* is a popular divertissement.

The Red Poppy. Music by Glière, choreography Tikhomirov. Kirov Theatre, 1927. A new version by Lavrovsky at the Bolshoi Theatre, 1949 (Ulanova as Ta Hor).

(A story of colonialist exploitation in China.)

Taras Bulba. Music by Soloviev-Sedoi, choreography Lopokov. Kirov Theatre, 1940. (Inspired by Gogol's novel.)

FOKINE BALLETS FIRST PRODUCED FOR DIAGHILEV

(To be seen in England and now in the Soviet Union)

Les Sylphides. (In Russia, *Chopiniana*). Music Chopin. (Nocturne op 32, No. 2, Valse, op 70, No. 1, Mazurka op 33, No. 2, Mazurka op 76, No. 3, Prelude, op 28, No. 7, Valse op 64, No. 2, Valse op 18, No. 1.) A romantic reverie with choreography by Michael Fokine, décors by Alexandre Benois. First given at a charity performance in St Petersburg in 1908 and given the following year in Paris with Pavlova, Karsavina and Nijinsky. (See text page 71.)

The Firebird. Music by Stravinsky, ballet and choreography by Fokine, décors by Golovine and in later productions by Gontcharova. First given in Paris in 1910 with Karsavina and A. Bolm.

There have been revivals by Balanchine with décors by Chagal 1949 and by Lifar with décors by Wakhevitch 1954. The original was revived by the Sadler's Wells Ballet for the Edinburgh Festival, 1954.

Petrouchka. Music by Stravinsky, choreography by Fokine, book and décors by Benois. First presented in 1911 with Karsavina, Nijinsky, Orlov and Cecchetti. Has been revived by many companies with a number of different décors by A. Benois. Revived by the Royal Ballet in 1957. (See text page 90 et seq.)

Le Spectre de la Rose. Music by Weber (l'Invitation à la Valse), ballet by Jean Louis Vaudoyer after Gautier. Choreography by Fokine, décors by Bakst. First presented in 1911 (with Karsavina and Nijinsky). (See text page 76 et seq.)

Polovtsian dances from Prince Igor. Music by Borodin, choreography by Fokine, décors by Roerich. First produced in 1909 with A. Bolm and S. Fedorova.

This ballet played a great role in re-establishing the male dancer in Western Europe.

CONTEMPORARY ONE ACT BALLETS

Ballet Imperial. Music by Tchaikovsky (2nd piano concerto), choreography by Balanchine, 1941.

Revived at Covent Garden, 1950.

A neo-classical ballet with no narrative.

Checkmate. Music by Arthur Bliss, book by Arthur Bliss. Choreography Nineitte de Valois. Décors E. McKnight Kauffer. First given in Paris, 1937, by Sadler's Wells Ballet.

Has been given in Vienna, Ankara and elsewhere.

(A game of chess as a symbol of life and death.)

Façade. Music by William Walton, written originally to accompany poems by Edith Sitwell. Choreography by Frederick Ashton. Created for the Camargo Society, 1931.

In the repertoire of The Royal Ballet and the Rambert Ballet. (A suite de danses in which the dance laughs at itself.)

Hamlet. Music by Tchaikovsky, choreography by Robert Helpmann, décors by Leslie Hurry.

First performed by Sadler's Wells Ballet, 1942,

(Describes the dying thoughts of Hamlet from a Freudian point of view.)

Les Patineurs. Music by Meyerbeer, selected by Lambert from *Le Prophète* and *L'Étoile du Nord,* choreography by Frederick Ashton. First performed by Sadler's Wells Ballet, 1937.

(A 'skating' suite de danses.)

The Rake's Progress. Music by Gavin Gordon, choreography Ninette de Valois, décors Rex Whistler (after Hogarth).

First produced by the Sadler's Wells Ballet, 1935.

(Inspired by Hogarth's famous paintings.)

Sérénade. Music by Tchaikovsky (*Serenade for Strings*), choreography by Balanchine. First produced in 1934 and since revived in repertoires in France and England.

A non-story ballet but in no sense abstract.

INDEX

155

INDEX

156

INDEX

157

INDEX